Life on the Track:
Memoirs of a Socialist Worker

Frank Henderson
Afterword by Matt Perry

LIFE ON THE TRACK
memoirs of a socialist worker

frank henderson
afterword by matt perry

Life on the Track: Memoirs of a Socialist Worker
Frank Henderson
Afterword by Matt Perry

First published in January 2009 by Bookmarks Publications
Copyright © Bookmarks Publications

ISBN 978-1905192465

Typeset by Bookmarks Publications
Printed by BookPrintingUK.com

Cover photograph: Mass meeting at Longbridge, 1970s.

Thanks to *Socialist Worker* archive for cover photograph and images of
Socialist Worker and to the Modern Records Library, Warwick University
for images of *Carworker*, *Socialist Appeal* and the *Edwardes Plan* pamphlet.

Contents

About this book

This book was a product of interviews between Frank Henderson and Matt Perry. Matt also contributed the Notes at the end of the book. He is Reader in Labour History at Newcastle University. He is the author of *Prisoners of Want: The Experience and Protest of the Unemployed in France, 1921-45* (Ashgate, 2007), *The Jarrow Crusade: Protest and Legend* (University of Sunderland Press, 2005), and *Bread and Work: The Experience of Unemployment, 1918-39* (Pluto, 2000).

Preface

The Russian revolutionary Leon Trotsky characterised a revolution as a situation where the masses enter the stage of history. Frank Henderson's life suggests that what defines a revolutionary is the permanent entry onto that stage, an unceasing engagement with great events, albeit as a minor part of the supporting cast. Frank directly experienced the Coventry blitz, the Second World War in Italy and Greece where he encountered the partisan movements, the last days of British rule in Palestine, the early days of Algerian independence and the miners' victory at Saltley Gates in 1972. He was part of the revolutionary left during the Second World War, called up into the British army, a Labour councillor when that party was a mass organisation delivering reforms, and a Longbridge shop steward during the heyday of trade union militancy. With a keen political awareness from his adolescence, his reminiscences record how great events—the Hitler-Stalin Pact, the Dunkirk spirit, the Churchill myth, the foundation of Israel, the Hungarian Revolution of 1956, the IRA's Birmingham pub bombings—touched an ordinary person in indirect and even quirky ways. To introduce his life is to introduce some of the most momentous times of the 20th century.

CHAPTER ONE

Youth

Early life and family traditions

I was born in Wolverhampton in Stevenson Street near to Chapel Ash which runs into St Marks Street.[1] When I was six or seven we moved to Coventry. They were old, late-Victorian terraced houses in Wolverhampton. My father worked at Orme Evans. The factory was just over the road. He only had to get out of bed and he was working. The job didn't last as long as any of the houses. It was mainly producing sheet metal products—teapots, coffee pots, billy cans. I think they extended the range after the First World War. He was a sheet metal worker, and a good one. What he did—possibly out of having such a large family—was chase the highest wage in the district. So quite often when he found himself living in Wolverhampton he would chase over to Coventry because he could get a job that paid more money.

Orme Evans was a typical factory of the period—an extension of the individual craft and moving towards more standardised forms of production, but nowhere near the same level as the car industry in Coventry. One of the reasons for the decline in the motor industry in Wolverhampton was that the older premises didn't lend themselves to mass production. So skilled men, in particular, travelled away and moved to Coventry or possibly Birmingham in the 1930s to get jobs in the aircraft industry as well as the motor plants. There has been a lot of talk about why companies such as Austin and Morris got the financial backing to move to mass production. In the inter-war years the Star, the Sun, the Clino were all established names in Wolverhampton. But the reality was that these were produced by little factories hemmed in by streets, with no possibility for real expansion, whereas there were green-field sites available in Coventry, Birmingham and Oxford to expand production lines. That is why the motor industry moved to those places, and so did the men. It was skilled rather than semi-skilled men who made the move. Although the new production lines were supposed to eliminate skilled men, it did not work out quite like that. There was still an extraordinary amount of skill required for quite a number of jobs. It was certainly worth the employers' money to employ a skilled worker rather than try to train a man from scratch. The situation is different now, with pressing techniques that make it easier.

My father's attitude was that he wouldn't work for anything other than the top rate in the district. It didn't matter whether he was working in a place where knew the gaffer, perhaps had worked for the gaffer 20 years ago and knew it was a nice, comfortable little job. If there was a penny or tuppence an hour more being paid at another place, he would not work for anything other than the top rate.

He was proud of his skills, but he didn't allow this to affect his judgement on what was needed in terms of solidarity on the part of trade unionists and the working class. He was in the National Union of Sheet Metal Workers, which began as a series of small local organisations. There was the Birmingham Sheet Metal Workers Society, the Wolverhampton Tinsmiths' Society, the London Society of Tinsmiths and so on. These went through a process of amalgamation immediately after the First World War, and merged to form the National Union of Sheet Metal Workers. There was one exception—and that was the biggest, strongest and richest society—the Birmingham and Midland Society, which remained aloof mainly to hold on to its funds. But, in general, relations between the two unions were reasonable at the shopfloor level, anyway. There was a lot of squabbling on the part of the officials. These kept their eyes fixed firmly on the funds—as officials have always done—and that was always a cause of disagreement. But it rolled off the backs of the workers on the shopfloor, who never saw the funds once they had paid their dues.

There were certainly traditions of militancy among the craft unions, particularly the sheet metal workers. But, in the main, they were traditions of craft-based militancy based on defending their own little pitch against any invasion. The reputation for militancy exceeded the occasions it happened, although I found the skilled workers never hesitated if they thought strike action was necessary.

Coventry and the engineering boom of the 1930s

There was a high level of unemployment generally in the 1930s, but in areas like Birmingham and Coventry, where new industries such as the motor and aircraft industries were developing, there was still a call for skilled men. And sheet metal workers took full advantage of that.

I remember as a kid things were hard generally speaking. But with my father being a skilled man and having a lot of sons approaching working age, we didn't do too badly. Certainly, we never had the level of toys and things at Christmas that kids look forward to now. But we didn't do too bad.

My mother and eldest sister stopped at home. You're talking of a family of 12 kids. There was more work than one woman could ever cope with.

I was seven when we moved over to Coventry and almost 16 when we came away. Constantly during that time new factories and new houses were built at a rapid pace. I think we lived in five different houses in Coventry and there was building going on around all of them. I remember one house where we lived had got the name "Ruin View" because you could see the ruins of a medieval castle—Caludon Castle. It was on the Ansty Road about a mile from where the Walsgrave Hospital is now. Walsgrave was a sleepy little village in 1932. Then it was just swamped. In the space of a few years the view from our house had become ruined because they built a whole estate around it.

What had been the heart of the countryside had become houses. In other parts of Coventry, around the edges of the town, there had been a tremendous expansion of factories. The Standard Motor factory in Cambley had an 18-hole golf course which was developed as a plant, heavily subsidised by the government for aircraft parts. As the war got nearer, later in the 1930s, a series of factories were built stretching right out through Tile Hill. Anyone involved in the aircraft industry or motor industry built a place near Coventry. I remember at Standard, when they built the shadow factory on the old golf course the local paper interviewed the managing director who went by the name of Black and asked him, "How do you expect to get the labour to keep the factory going as there is no unemployment near the site?"[2] "No problem, if I want the labour I'll just pay more than anybody else," he said. That is exactly what he did. He was thrown out of the Engineers Employers Federation as a result. But that wasn't just the attitude of Black. It was the attitude of employers in the Coventry area. It was a boom town based on cars and aircraft and if employers wanted the labour they could pay to get it. In the aircraft industry as often as not it was government money being paid out.

The new employers—the Black family who ran the Standard Motor Company, Herbert Austin at Longbridge and Nuffield (Morris at it was then) in Cowley—did everything they could to stop the growth of trade unions. One of my older brothers worked at Standard and got the sack for selling the *New Propellor* which was the Communist Party's aircraft shop stewards' paper.[3] It was a very good rank and file paper. This brother of mine had never been involved with the Communist Party, but he was certainly involved in selling the paper and he got the sack for doing it. By the time the war had gone on for 12 months, victory had been won as far as unionisation was concerned and the employers had to accept it whether they liked it or not. The brother who got the sack was Bill, who died a couple of years ago. He had no problems getting work again because of the full employment.

School days

We were a Catholic family in so far as my mother was a Catholic. My father wasn't. He was a Protestant, but religion never really played any role. Going to Catholic schools, we were more or less forced into going to church but no real pressure came from my parents. I think as far as my father was concerned he would let us make up our own minds but if we made up our minds to be anti-church that was how he would like it. I went to church while I was at school. I had to, otherwise I'd get the cane. But I don't think I ever went to church after I left school apart from the odd funeral.

Practically all the education I had was in Coventry. The school I went to for most of the time was a little Catholic school with seven classes. In the infants' school sometimes there were two classes for one room. The male teachers took the senior teaching jobs almost automatically and the women took the junior jobs. We hated the headmaster. He was a bully and a snob and used to enjoy walloping us with a cane. I always got the feeling his one regret was that he wasn't allowed to cane the girls and had to send them to the women teachers, who hated the idea of caning so any punishment administered to the girls was derisory. It wasn't derisory to us boys. They were pretty selective about who they caned and I was a recipient on a number of occasions. I don't think I ever really liked giving way to authority. I was always likely to start arguing the toss. It's a bit like being in the army. Once you'd been on a charge and the sergeant-major knew your face, you were always on a charge. If anybody was going to get the cane it was going to be me. But all it did was harden me up. The authorities wanted to impose discipline so I'd do as I was told without question. But what it did was instill in me an instinctive dislike of authority and a readiness to rebel at any opportunity.

Having said that, I enjoyed my school years. We had a good football team. We used to deal with bullying in our own way. If we found anybody bullying, we didn't think it was necessary to report it them to the police or parents or anybody. If we caught anybody bullying we sorted them out and, once we sorted them out, they never went in for bullying again. It was a real good time. I think I preferred maths overall. We had one teacher—Bill Coll—who taught maths, who was a good teacher. Somehow or other he actually enjoyed teaching. Don't ask me why. What it did was brush off on us—a concept as old fashioned now as it was then. The one subject I didn't like—but I've got interested in since—was history. All we did was learn the dates of accession to the throne of the various

Plantagenets and so on. Occasionally the teacher would branch out to explain Britain had never been defeated in a war and then we would discuss the Saxons and the Romans and all the rest of it. That particular teacher was totally ignorant—hadn't got a clue what he was talking about. Subjects that could be interesting would be boring and dull. It took going out and working for a living to rekindle my interest in history. He was the sort of idiot, this senior teacher, that we would do poetry and his idea of poetry was that we all had to memorise a poem and he'd pick kids at random to get up and repeat their poem. The idea was, of course, to find the shortest poem you could, to jump up, gabble it out and finish. On one occasion I remember I did something a bit different. Instead of coming out with something like *Patriot* by Robert Lewis Stephenson,[4] for some reason I memorised the soliloquy of Mark Anthony over the dead body of Julius Caesar. I think I did it mainly so I could get the word "bleeding" in—"this bleeding piece of earth". But he gave me the stick for not learning a piece of poetry and he came out with the classic, "The only poetry Shakespeare wrote was his sonnets. All the rest was merely blank verse." "Merely blank verse" is not how I would describe most of Shakespeare's work.

Introduction to politics

I was at when school Edward VIII abdicated. Our teacher was solidly in favour of the abdication and of King George, so the kids voted in favour of King Edward VIII. That was our protest against the teacher.[5] I remember during the general election of 1931 going round the streets—we were still in Wolverhampton then—with dustbin lids banging them with a stick: "Vote for Mr Brown." There was a Brown and a Bird. Brown was the Labour candidate and Bird, the custard man, was the Tory. We had fights about it. It had nothing to do with politics. It was just a question of pitting ourselves in a convenient sized gang to make the fighting worthwhile.

I was still a school kid when war was declared. Since the Munich episode in 1938 everybody seemed to accept war was inevitable.[6] When I say that, as far as I can recall the political leaders were always talking of peace being possible. But among ordinary people there was a general recognition that war was coming. Even allowing for the hypocrisy of political leaders, ordinary people had a better understanding than the politicians. When war was declared I was torn between dismay that I was too young—fearing, "It'll all be over before I can involve myself"—and a feeling that, bearing in mind what happened in the First World War, this might be the best thing for me. There were warring emotions in my teenage heart.

First job

I left school at 14 at Easter 1939 and went to work at a little place making—of all things—batteries for hen incubators. It was hard graft and non-union. It was a small place and I was working in galvanised iron, learning how to solder it. To solder galvanised iron you had to burn the zinc off with raw hydrochloric acid, which creates all sorts of fumes. You breathe it in and it rips your guts out. It was pretty rough, but it taught me how to work and I learned quite a bit from there. It was exacting work and quite skilled and I learned a lot.

I left there after seven or eight months and went to work at another small place where my old man was working at the time, where the main job was making delousers for the army. They were made up of three cylinders of galvanised iron separated by corks and other insulating materials. The soldiers' uniforms were put in for cleaning and steaming to delouse them. It was awkward to do all the soldering necessary inside those cylinders. Whoever was doing the soldering had to bend right inside, with no escaping from the fumes, from the sulphuric acid used to burn the zinc off. You had to learn to control your breathing more than any opera singer. That was one big job. There were other jobs that were not so harmful, a lot more interesting and, possibly, a lot more skilled. Of course, when I went there, following tradition I was what they called a shop boy. That was just a gopher. You made the tea for the blokes. Any errand that needed running, you'd do it. Anything that wanted fetching and carrying, you fetched it and so on. But after a

few months the gaffer found out that I had worked at the other
place and knew how to solder galvanised iron, so he wanted me
soldering galvanised iron because there was always a shortage.
Nobody wanted that job.

Even though it was a small place, it was paying higher wages
than bigger plants in Coventry, probably because of the conditions.
The gaffer knew I could do this soldering, but before I could do it I
had to be in the union—and before you could be in the union you
had to be 16. I was only just 15. So we had quite a few arguments
about it and in the end the gaffer raised it with the union officials
who sorted out a compromise. I was summonsed in front of the
branch committee who questioned me and decided I could be in the
union but that I had to be 16 officially, which meant that I would
have to accept an increase in wages from 12/6 a week to 28/6 a
week. I reluctantly accepted this! My old man was a member of the
branch committee at the time, but he went out of the room when
they were discussing my case. Anyway I had my rise and I did a bit
of sheet metal work there. My name went down to go to the technical college. As part of the apprenticeship you had to go to technical
college in the evenings. The union paid for the first year's tuition
fees. I think it was 12/6 or something like that but, low and behold,
just when that was all fixed up aircraft started coming over and
dropping bombs and the course was cancelled. I and so many others
who should have been going to technical college found ourselves
free in the evenings. Those bombers certainly saved us some school.

CHAPTER TWO

War and the revolutionary

The Coventry blitz and the "Dunkirk spirit"

There was a series of air raids during the summer and autumn of 1940 that increased in intensity—the night raids—until the night of 14-15 November. It was the first all-night blitz on Coventry. We came back to Wolverhampton after that. We felt that—with half the windows in the house blown out, half the slates blown off the roof, a delayed-action bomb in the front garden—moving back to Wolverhampton wasn't a bad idea. One of the casualties of that night's bombing was the place where I worked. Most of it was blown in. Being under 16, I didn't come under the essential works order so, when my family moved back to Wolverhampton, I had to go with them. But anyone over 16 had to stop where they were working. So my elder brothers and father had to stay in Coventry to work while the rest of us went to Wolverhampton. There was no problem getting a job in Wolverhampton, of course.

The first event that really had any impact in Britain, that they tried to portray as a great victory, was the scuttling of the *Graf Spee*.[1] Churchill tried to lead all the pomp and fury when dealing with this "great and marvellous victory", but it didn't really affect anybody. The first thing to have a major impact was the invasion of Norway. There was a general feeling of amazement that there could be such a great cock-up.[2] It was whispered that it was wrong to land thousands of troops on the coast of one part of Norway and then send all their supplies to another coast 200 miles away.

Things moved rapidly to the fall of France and Dunkirk. I don't know much about the Dunkirk spirit. We never noticed it much. It was a question of resignation, waiting to see what was going to happen next. Nobody accepted what is now the official version of Dunkirk, that they organised a fleet of small boats to fetch the troops off the beaches of Dunkirk.[3] What really happened was that ordinary people got hold of boats and took them over and did it in defiance rather than in response to any sort of leadership.

Generally speaking, people were numbed at the time. There was that much happening. The tendency was just to sit tight and see how things developed. I never noticed any upsurge in patriotism. I was in Coventry and what had most effect on people's attitude to the war was the bombing. Everybody thinks of Coventry being flattened by one big raid but in fact there was a whole series of raids during the summer and autumn leading up to that. Even this didn't necessarily have the effect of reinforcing patriotic ideas. But it did convince people that, whether they liked it or not, Hitler and the Nazis had to be destroyed. There was a genuine hatred of the Nazis, not just as a reaction to the bombing, but because there had built up since before the war this hatred for the ideas of fascism and Nazism. It was a genuine hatred.

I can't recall ever meeting anybody who had anything decent to say about Chamberlain or Halifax.[4] One or two people might mutter that Anthony Eden wasn't as bad, but that was limited.[5] There was a general dislike of the Tories, certainly among the working class, who considered that it wasn't just a question of Chamberlain being an appeaser. The Conservatives were considered to be linked to the Nazis, linked to the fascists, if not in any formal sense then in terms of sharing a great deal of the same ideology. So people could hate the Tories and still accept Churchill. The general impression I had of people's attitude to Churchill was that they disliked or even hated him because of his anti working class and anti trade union attitudes. People still remembered the General Strike when he edited the *British Worker* that attacked ordinary working people as the enemy. The working class still tended to regard him as the enemy in the 1940s and they remembered him as the "butcher of Tonypandy"—an episode historians have since tried to whitewash.[6] But they tended to accept Churchill as a war leader on the basis that when you're involved in such a war possibly the best leader you can have is a warmonger. Come the peace, people thought, we shall take the first chance we get to get rid of him and the rest of the Tories. That is why in the 1945 general election the Tories suffered a landslide defeat. Churchill was elected as Tory MP for Woodford, Essex, in 1945 only because the other main parties did not oppose him. If the Labour Party had stood, he would have been out of parliament. However, his only challenger was a candidate who stood because he thought no MP should be elected unopposed.[7] That seemed to be the general attitude among the working class. People were generally anti-Tory, anti-boss.

The newspapers were restricted in how much paper they used and all gave the official Ministry of Information version of what took place. The *Daily Mirror* occasionally made a few criticisms of the government, but these were muted and hardly ranked as criticism to someone like me. There were a few critical cartoons which seemed to get up the noses of Herbert Morrison and Labour, more than anyone else.[8] It seemed the Tories didn't give a sod what people said about them as long as they called the tune. The Labour cabinet members—Attlee, Morrison, Bevin—were constantly having to justify their acceptance of government positions so they were sensitive to all sorts of criticism. They reacted in what can only be described as stupid ways such as Herbert Morrison not only banning the *Daily Worker*, but following it up by threatening to ban the *Daily Mirror*. In fact, I think even at that time the *Daily Mirror* was more powerful than Herbert Morrison if it had come to a test of strength. But it showed how sensitive they were about having to serve with these warmongers in the cabinet.

Generally speaking, people regarded strikes as something to be avoided during the war. It wasn't an outright condemnation of strikes, but they accepted you only went on strike as an absolute last resort to get problems sorted out. But although they tended to accept that on a generalised theoretical level, when it came to their own workplace, workers would say if there is a strike here it's not our fault; it's the bloody boss's fault. We're only going on strike because we've been provoked and pushed into it. They could accept the call for no strike action in a generalised way, but they were still ready to fight back. It has to be said that in 99 cases out of 100 if it came to an argument they could win without having to go on strike because it didn't hurt the employers to any great extent. So many employers were involved in government work and being paid on the cost-plus system, all the costs of production plus a 10 percent profit margin. This gave them the opportunity to falsely boost the costs. So the cost of producing a bullet might be a penny, but by the time it had reached the government it was tuppence. The 10 percent became 20 percent and so on. Every now and then, if it came to a push, they could allow a little bit of that to swing back to the workforce. There is no doubt most places saw an upsurge in wages during the war, partly due to being able to negotiate better prices on piecework jobs and better bonuses on a localised basis, ignoring any attempts by the national union leadership to negotiate national levels of wages. At most, that just affected holiday pay and so on. Generally, problems could be sorted out at a local level and that is the way it was done with a few exceptions.

The Beveridge Report was a response to this leftward feeling among working people in Britain.[9] All sorts of measures were adopted to prove that the war was worthwhile—"We'll all stick together", "We're all in the same boat," and, "We all share the same views." I saw it at the time—the Beveridge Report—as just another sop in this direction. When the report is talked about even in left wing circles as a blueprint for the welfare state it is sheer nonsense. I have heard people talk of the National Health Service as though it depended on Beveridge. Beveridge's idea of a national health service was that it would be a nationally insured health service. If you weren't insured, you would not get the health service. It would have been a question of pay first and lucky if you get anything afterwards. The idea of the National Health Service that met with universal approval from the working class after the war completely rejected insurance contributions. Rather it was paid for directly out of taxation and free to anybody—irrespective of whether they were insured—when they needed treatment. Most people were cynical about it. I saw it as a sop to try to alleviate any pressure for a real socialist at the time.

Socialist ideas

When I got a job in Wolverhampton, it was at Midlands Metal Spinning. It had a little section engaged in aircraft work. The section was all unionised, whereas the rest weren't. It had a shop committee and the chair was a bloke called Terry Finn who lived in Mason Street. He had built himself a beautiful aluminum bookcase alongside his working area and had a collection of Penguin and Pelican books.[10] He used to hire them out at a penny a time and operate a little library. He was a member of the ILP, used to be a Clarion cyclist and delighted in listening to Lord Haw-Haw and Radio Moscow on a beautiful big cabinet wireless.[11] You could get the news in English from Moscow. I used to pop around occasionally and listen to it in the process of reading these books. I read Sir Mortimer Wheeler's *Ur of the Chaldees* and various archaeological things, but 70 percent-80 percent of them dealt with politics in one way or another. The socialism he was fond of never really stuck me as particularly great. He was fond of H.G. Wells and I liked H.G. Wells, but when he was writing science fiction. I didn't mind *War of the Worlds* and *The Invisible Man*, but when it came to discussing socialism, he seemed on the weak side.[12] For Wells, it was a matter of persuading the ruling class that they would be better off under socialism. It struck me that, if the ruling class is better off under socialism, what the hell is the bloody point of it to the working class? But, nevertheless, we used to have arguments over socialism and I read an enormous number of his Penguins and Pelicans to the extent that I joined the ILP. It wasn't an easy thing for him to hold to the position of being anti-war.

The Independent Labour Party

I joined the ILP at the beginning of 1941.[13] I think my first involvement in activity was at a screening Charlie Chaplin's anti-Hitler film, *The Great Dictator*, at the Savoy cinema in Wolverhampton. I think the film could have been shown earlier, but the distributors

wouldn't distribute it because they thought it might cause diplomatic problems.[14] But during the war, of course, it was okay.
Anyway, we went along. The significant thing about that film, apart
from taking the mickey out of Hitler and the Nazis, was that it was
the first film in which Charlie Chaplin spoke.[15] At the end of the
film he gave an impassioned plea for honesty and freedom and
brotherly care for each other, for a world of peace and goodness.
The ILP reproduced this speech in leaflet form and my introduction
to public activity was to stand outside the Savoy and distribute
copies of Charlie Chaplin's speech.[16] That was a fairly easy thing to
start with. Some of the things we sold later got a bit hard. I was
always grateful I was blooded on something soft and simple like
that, and ever after I appreciated Charlie Chaplin. I don't think
much of his speech in terms of political content. But in terms of
being anti-Nazi and anti-Hitler, it was acceptable.

The ILP at the time seemed split down the middle: half opposed
the war and half supported it. Then again, of the half that opposed
the war, half of them did so because they were pacifists under any
circumstances and the other half did so on political grounds—
opposing an imperialist government engaged in an imperialist war.
So there were all these arguments going on in the ILP. We used to
have some good and interesting meetings and some boring. I was
impressed by the courage of some of the people. I remember two
members registered as conscientious objectors on political grounds
and finished up in Stafford jail. The others started taking lessons
from bookbinders because you were allowed to give the prisoners
one book a month. One book a month isn't much good if you're
incarcerated, so we used to get four or five books and bind them
into one and there would be one huge book to take each month. In
a six-month sentence, you would get a good library. They were prepared to go to jail for their principles and that gained my respect.

But my politics advanced a bit further. Around Easter 1941 I
went to a conference in Birmingham called by the ILP and chaired
by Barry Cadbury of Cadbury's chocolates—a Quaker and a pacifist. The conference was called on the question, what can we do to
stop the war? I went as a delegate from Wolverhampton. When I
got there I was confronted with people selling this paper *Youth for*

Socialism.[17] I bought the paper, had a bit of an argument with the sellers, went inside to the conference and found myself sitting next to a guy called Percy Downey. He was a member of the ILP, but he'd also joined the Workers' International League, a Trotskyist organisation, and we got to arguing the toss afterwards. I found the ideas put over by the Workers' International League tuned in to my ideas, not just about what socialism is, but how to get it. In a short space of time I joined the WIL. My brother had also gone through a similar experience and also joined in Coventry. It wasn't until he came over to Wolverhampton that I found out.

The books that really impressed me were the bread-and-butter Marxist books. I've still got them upstairs—Little Lenin Library published by the Communist Party. They also had the Marxist-Leninist library, which comprised bigger books. I found I could read the short Lenin pamphlets and learn something from them: *State and Revolution, Socialism and War, Left-Wing Communism.* Then I thought I'd better get down to reading the real stuff and I bought *The Poverty of Philosophy* by Marx. I hadn't a clue. I struggled and struggled and eventually gave it up. I've read it since. I know a little more now. But I hadn't a clue then, I have to admit. Looking back, if I'd stuck to the *Communist Manifesto*, I'd have done better. Among all the reading I did at that time probably the book that had more influence on me than anything else was Marx's *The Civil War in France.* It's always struck me as the most wonderful example of revolutionary journalism in which he commentates on what's going on and analyses it at the same time. He sees what's happening, the progress they're making, how they organise, who's doing it, the mistakes they make, and draws lessons from it. If I am called on to recommend books as an introduction to Marxism, I would say the *Communist Manifesto* and *The Civil War in France.* The funny thing is that once I had an insight from reading the easier books by Marx, I found I could read *Value, Price and Profit* (as it was called then), and *Wage-Labour and Capital.* They came relatively easy and, having absorbed them, you could start talking in terms of *The Poverty of Philosophy* and not be completely lost.

The big problem we had during the war was getting hold of books. The Trotskyist movement was so isolated that what books there were were printed, in the main, in the US and were almost impossible to get over here. To get a book published in America I had to go to bookstall in Beatties [the Wolverhampton department store], order the book and pay them the money cash down and then they would order it from America. But there was no such thing as insurance. If the ship went down, the book went down. If they couldn't be bothered to send it, there was no proof. You were taking a big gamble ordering books. The charges were enormous really, for an apprentice. I read some of the Left Book Club stuff.[18] At that time it was only occasional copies you got hold of. I wasn't a member of the Left Book Club and by then it was fading out. What killed it was Russia entering the war. They were still pushing out popular front stuff during the war, like Norman Angell, but nothing really invigorating or new.[19]

I remember having a great search to get a copy of *Ten Days That Shook the World*.[20] The Communist Party had originally decided to print it. They had the book printed and then withdrew it when they found it so contrary to the line. The book keeps mentioning Trotsky and not mentioning Stalin. So they stopped selling it, destroyed the books they had and tried to get back by fair means or foul every copy that had been sold. I was told there were only about half a dozen copies circulating in Britain and one of them, by some stroke of fortune, belonged to a man who lived in Wolverhampton on the Willenhall Road, a man by the name of Trubshaw. I tracked him down and went to see him. We nearly came to blows and he wouldn't let me have the book. He was a guy who'd been attracted to Trotskyism before the war, but couldn't stand the isolation when the war started. If you were a Trotskyist, and you let people know you were a Trotskyist, you were likely to get beaten up by Stalinists. It's not easy and comfortable if you're on your own. So he had backed away from politics although still inside he still believed in it—though he wouldn't do anything in terms of pushing the ideas forward. The net result was that I didn't get to read *Ten Days that Shook the World*, but I did get a regular sale for *Socialist Appeal*. And that was about it. Books were always a problem and that was where the old saying arose—you could trust a Trotskyist with your life, but never with a book. We used to have to borrow and beg and it's astonishing how people used to mislay them.

When I moved away from Midland Metal Spinning in late 1941, I went to work at ICI. Kay Brutton, a leading member of the local Communist Party, was working near me. We got on quite well together. He was anti-war, and I was anti-war. He was anti-imperialist, and I was anti-imperialist. I'd got ideas that Trotsky might be alright, but I was only a young kid, and they'd knock those silly ideas out of my head later on. I never joined the Communist Party—I regarded them even in those days as degenerate Stalinists. What I did do was go along to the *Labour Monthly* discussion groups. The CP published this theoretical journal every month and they opened up with the "Notes of the Month" by the editor, Palme Dutt. Each person who attended would take it in turns to introduce a discussion based on these "Notes". I used to go along and we would have some reasonable discussions. But then came June 22 and Hitler invaded Russia.[21] As it happened, I was due to lead the discussion at the July meeting and, of course, the Communist Party line changed. Suddenly you became a fascist sympathiser if you opposed the war and anti-patriotic if you didn't support Churchill. Among the ultra-patriots there was nothing to beat the Communist Party once they got moving, and it didn't take them long to get moving.

When the July meeting of the *Labour Monthly* discussion group was due to take place relations were a bit strained, but I went along to open the discussion. Nobody there. I waited for a long time. Nobody came. I went down to where I knew Kay Brutton lived on the Merridale Road. No one there. I had to give up in the end. Later I found out that they had circulated everybody they thought was liable to go, even might possibly go, and told them the meeting was being held in a pub at the other end of the town. But they didn't tell me. That was my first introduction to how they operated. But that was the easiest way they operated. We—myself and my brother—found ourselves denounced as Hitler's agents, disrupters, saboteurs and so on. Looking back, it seems absurd they could go to these lengths denouncing a 16 year old kid. In retrospect it is ridiculous but it wasn't ridiculous in those times. It wasn't easy to be denounced. The CP even put leaflets round the factory where we worked—two leaflets denouncing Trotskyists: "Clear out Hitler's agents" being one and a more theoretical version of the same thing written, I think, by Ted Bramley, the district organiser.[22] The local Communist Party got one of these John Bull rubber sets and stamped my name on the leaflet as Hitler's local agent.

Workers' International League (WIL)

The Workers' International League was a lot more serious than the ILP which was split down the middle over the war. Formally, a majority opposed it. The three ILP MPs opposed the war in parliament. But the ILP theoretical journal came under the editorship of Dr C A Smith who was pro-war. Even among those opposed to the war there was a series of splits. There were those who opposed it on pacifist grounds, and the pacifists split between Christian pacifists, moral pacifists, rational pacifists and others who argued the war was an imperialist war and working people should have nothing to do with it.

But the tendency, even among those who put a formally correct view of it being an imperialist war, was to stop short of taking the argument any further. It was alright condemning the war as imperialist, but people wanted to know what you were going to do about it: what did you propose? So we put forward proposals that the fight against fascism and the Nazis could take place as part of the struggle against imperialism and capitalism. This was never really touched on by the ILP, whereas with the WIL everything was directed towards that aim. Our programme always started with a call for a return of Labour to power on the basis of a socialist programme. A socialist programme meant nationalisation and getting out of the colonies—a generalised anti-capitalist and anti-imperialist programme. The ILP as a party would pass pronunciations condemning the war—and, let's be fair, MPs Jimmy Maxton, Campbell Steven and John McGovern made speeches opposing the war—but the ILP as an organisation couldn't really do anything because of the number of splits they accepted. I'm in favour, in any organisation, of a massive amount of argument and debate, but within the bounds of generally accepted aims. The argument about whether you support or are against an imperialist war seems to me to be such a divide that you can't contain the two sides of the argument. What happened with the ILP very much depended on local activity and attitudes of people locally. There were some ILP branches that were under the control of Trotskyists. They made quite useful interventions.

What we did in the ILP was scavenge on other organisations, and we did this in the WIL as well. Whenever the Communists called a meeting, or the liberals, whoever called a meeting, we would sell the *New Leader* or various pamphlets.[23] For example, Oliver Brown wrote a pamphlet, *War for Freedom or Finance,* and in a series of paragraphs exposed what was happening when it came to profiteering out of the war.[24] He put the profiteering of the capitalist class in stark contrast to the verbal statements of sacrifice they were making and inviting the working class to make. We distributed and sold pamphlets and got quite a reasonable response. The Communist Party was vicious about us. I remember we used to meet in Market Patch, a centre for open air meetings. There was a guy who fancied himself as a leader and used to organise these outdoor meetings and explain what war was about to us ignorant masses. After the war he was a Labour councillor. The meetings used to be quite well attended. They were the only form of amusement available really. I remember on one occasion there must have been several hundred there and I was on the outskirts walking around selling *Socialist Appeal*. Half a dozen Communist Party members gathered around me as though they were having a talk and were that close that my elbows were stuck into my sides and I couldn't really move, and the one in front was carefully ripping up all my copies of the paper and scraped his army boots down my shins. It wasn't pleasant. I had youth on my side and when I started squealing there were a few people in the crowd who I thought were old, but they must have been middle aged, who turned on the CPers, saying, "Leave the boy alone!" If anything, I gained a little credibility.

I remember a few days afterwards being invited to go down to the police station and being interviewed by Sergeant Gwillam of

Special Branch, who pointed out that I if carried on doing things like that I could finish up being interned in the Isle of Man. I said, "Well if I live as luxuriously as Mosley while I'm there it won't be too bad." But he kept driving at me. I did nothing but tell him the strict truth, which he wouldn't believe. He wouldn't accept that the *Socialist Appeal* could be widely distributed around the area when there were only two people—me and my brother—who were actually involved with it. "Simply impossible," he said, "there must be a whole big branch of you, so who are the others?" A few weeks afterwards I had another call: "Would I go down to the police station to see Sergeant Gwillam?" He said, "There's a meeting next Monday on the Market Patch, isn't there?"

I said, "Yes."

He says, "Will you be there?"

I said "Yes."

"Will you be selling your papers?"

I said, "Yes."

I was waiting for him to tell me that if I did I would finish up on the Isle of Man. Instead he said, "Let me know details of when you intend to be there and how long you intend to stop and I'll ensure that you've got proper protection."

I said, "No, thank you, I prefer the protection of the class rather than cops."

I let it go at that, but periodically after he would bump into me and take me for a drink even when I was below the drinking age. I was always careful never to drink more than two half pints at public expense. He never learnt anything from me.

But the attitude of the Communist Party was really vile. I remember one meeting at the Aston Hippodrome in Birmingham where we were selling papers and the Stalinists organised to beat us up in a really disciplined and military fashion. They really did us. I remember afterwards we discussed what we could do. I was a bit naïve and suggested that we get the women to sell the papers because the Stalinists wouldn't attack the women members like they attacked us. We tried it, but the CP had no idea about sex discrimination. They beat up the women just the same as they beat up the men.

I remember at one meeting in Coventry, there must have been 3,000 there, and Harry Pollitt, the CP's general secretary, spoke. He spoke for an hour and must have spent three quarters of it trying to incite the crowd to do us for selling the paper. I don't think any of us were beat up that time. People simply wouldn't do it in Coventry. I think Coventry was probably the most advanced town in the country at the time. The first time I ever saw Trotskyist literature was in Coventry in 1940. I saw *Workers' International News* on sale in the Market Patch and I bought it to see what it was. The headline was "Stalin's Butcher Murders Trotsky"—this was the end of August 1940.[25] But I hadn't got a clue who Trotsky was and I didn't really follow the arguments at the time. That was my introduction to it.

The revolutionary paper

The papers were sent by post. We had 50 in Wolverhampton and usually sold them. Sometimes we'd fall a bit short and sometimes we'd have to borrow a few off Birmingham. The papers went fairly easily. Among people who disagreed with us there was still that left wing feeling. They were prepared to listen, read what we had to say, even agree with it but say, "What can we do in the middle of a war?" And they would point at our scarcity of numbers. By that time my brother had been called up and there was me on my own, and a 17 year old on his own isn't really a strong representative of a revolutionary argument or a pole of attraction. But people were sympathetic enough and said, "You're right there, they are a bunch of bastards, but where do we go from here?"

The paper was broadsheet size. We always tried to a get a front page which was a bit of a banner. When America was sending troops over we had a front page with a big picture of a lynching and the paper went through a series of lynchings and how America treated black people. How was this defending democracy? Another one showed a series of pictures of the central committee of the Bolshevik Party in 1917 and showed there were just two survivors. One, of course, was Stalin. The other was Alexandra Kollontai, who was ambassador to Finland or something. I thought that was pretty effective.[26]

Ted Grant was editor and he always inclined to soar into the stratosphere at the slightest chance.[27] There was a little strike in Willenhall down the road at a foundry with only eight people involved. They went on strike for an increase in wages. The gaffer had managed, in spite of making a fortune, to keep them on the wages they were paid in 1938. I went and had a word with them. It wasn't much, but it was eight people who were prepared to go on strike. So I wrote a little report—couldn't have been more than 50 words. I was on holiday and spent a week down in London and handed this little report to Ted. He said, "That's the thing." And he started writing a report about the strike. This little strike of eight, the way he was writing it, was the start of the world revolution. Fortunately, Jock Haston would always manage to pull his feet back to the ground.[28] I found this continually with Ted. He was willing to shoot up into the stratosphere for the slightest reason. The world revolution was going to happen tomorrow or the day after at most. Haston, on the other hand, was a master tactician and a realist who knew where things were going and fortunately kept Ted in check.

But the paper generally was pretty good, a brilliant achievement at the time, particularly when you consider all newsprint was rationed. The ration you got was based on your pre-war sales, which might be alright for the *Daily Mirror* but the pre-war sales of *Socialist Appeal—Youth for Socialism* it was called—were about 200 a month of a duplicated A4 thing, so the ration wouldn't amount to anything. Jock Haston had managed to organise to get the tail ends of bits of rolls of all the newspapers from God knows where and we used to do a deal with the local fishmongers. We would swap bundles of paper we had collected in return for a few sheets of white paper and used that for printing. It was amazing really.

What happened in Birmingham, Coventry and Wolverhampton might not have been the picture in Newcastle or Glasgow but generally we didn't have a street sale. The general argument we had against street sales was that they were a bit too haphazard. The paper was precious and we wanted to aim it in the right direction.

We wanted to: a) sell to people already interested in and arguing about politics, so at political meetings; and b) on workplace sales.

When I went down to London with the little report of that strike in Willenhall I was on holiday and that meant I could sell outside Hatfield's and de Havilland's [aircraft factories]. The problem was finding time to sell the paper because everybody was working seven days a week, 12 hours a day. If we'd had access to all the newsprint we could get we might have done street sales. As it was, we concentrated on workplace sales and sales at political meetings. Wherever we were it was taken for granted that you would be a member of a trade union, and that you would be the most active member of that union. You had to go to your branch meeting and you had to argue the toss. You had to sell the paper at the union meeting. You had to take on a shop steward's job if possible, which wasn't possible for me because they wouldn't allow you to be a steward unless you were 21 or over. We had an argument in our plant in Wolverhampton about allowing an apprentice to serve on the works committee. We finally won the day just before I was called up. Nationally, towards the end of the war, we formed the Militant Workers' Federation which was directed towards organising in industry, although I wasn't very involved.[29] It didn't really take off until 1944.

Wartime and the workplace

We were particularly powerful inside the Royal Ordnance factory in Nottingham, where there was a strong committee under the influence of the Workers' International League.[30] I think Al Richardson and Sammy Bornstein tend to go over the top a bit talking about this being the first example of workers' control in Britain, as though it was an isolated place that could exist separate from the rest of industry.[31] Trade unions are there to get the best out of the system, and if that means you take responsibility for this or that, OK. But you're still operating within the system. It wasn't really workers' control, but the works committee did really improve the level of earnings, the safety and the working conditions in the Ordnance factory in Nottingham and that spread to other factories. But it was the exception rather than the rule.

We had Sid Bidwell, who later became a Labour MP, as a member. He was a rail worker in Southall and had quite an influence there. A lot of the raw recruits were youngsters like myself, too young to compete for influential jobs in the trade union movement. Where we had influence was where someone had spent a period of years as a militant and built up a reputation.

I suppose the one exception was the apprentices' strike up on the Tyne where we managed to recruit Bill Davy, the secretary of the apprentices, and had some influence on the conduct of the strike.[32] This resulted in a great deal of antagonism—the worst I saw, on the one hand, from the Communist Party and, on the other, from the *Daily Mail*. I had a feeling at the time that, if the government had kept the ban on the *Daily Worker* and let the *Daily Mail* function as the official organ of the Communist Party, there would have been no problem. They ran this campaign against Trotskyist involvement in the strike. Eventually four members of the WIL went to jail. One of them, Ann Keen, had already been in prison for a couple of months before they decided a jail sentence was appropriate.[33] It gave us a great opportunity for a campaign and was as good an instance of the ruling class helping us out as we'd experienced up until then. People were listening to us, wanting to know who we were. A defence committee was organised.[34] Left wing Labour MPs appeared on the platform, acted as treasurers of the organisation, raised the question in parliament and so on. In the end the authorities more or less pushed the four out of jail so they could sweep it under the carpet.

There were no major disputes at my work. I found that most disputes could be settled on the basis of a threat and a compromise. The wages at the place where I was working in Wolverhampton were probably the highest in the area. It was only occasionally there was trouble and if anything did arise it was due to the stupidity of the gaffers irritating people. Usually the threat of action was enough to produce an apology.

Generally speaking, people tended to express support for strikes elsewhere without doing anything practical. The major strikes occurred in older industries. In the Midlands there were mainly new industries—cars and aircraft manufacturing. Because they were new, people were on better conditions than in the old-established industries like shipbuilding and mining. Trouble usually broke out in the older industries where the employers were trying to keep wages and conditions at the abysmal pre-war levels. In the newer industries workers started from several rungs higher on the ladder.

The Second Front

After Germany invaded the Soviet Union, ending the Hitler-Stalin pact, the Communist Party campaigned for Britain and America to open a second front against Nazi Germany. We opposed this. We never regarded it as part of our duty to advise the ruling class in Britain how to win their wars. The Communist Party couldn't accept the reason there wasn't a second front. The CP's allies Churchill and Roosevelt delayed a second front because they wanted Germany and Russia to tear the guts out of each other before stepping in. They saw their return to Europe as a mopping up operation in which they would dictate terms not only to Germany but also to Russia. A lot of people accepted our argument because they didn't want their relations involved in an assault like the D-Day landings. People are not going to advocate action that may result in their husbands or sons being killed. The Communist Party could do that, just as they could advocate scabbing on strikes for the sake of the Russian war effort.

Into the army

What action did I see? It can be summed up in one word: none. I was called up in 1944, missing the demand for troops in the Normandy landings. Shrewsbury is where Paul Foot went to improve his education and it's where I went to improve mine.[35] Only Paul went to the public school while I was called up to Copthorne Barracks. Nothing happened really. I had a hateful time in England before we were sent abroad, although one incident impressed. I was still selling one or two papers and was probably being ultra-secretive about it. While waiting to be sent abroad I was given the job of sweeping out the officers' rooms. We all lived in tents in the middle of a field, but the officers had rooms in this big house and I got to sweep up for them.

I went into one room to sweep up and what did I find? On the bedside table alongside the officer's bed, apart from a packet of 50 fags, there were about a dozen copies of *Socialist Appeal*, and it was the new edition that I hadn't received yet myself. So what did I do? I helped myself to one of his fags and picked up the paper. He came in to find me lying on his bed, smoking his fags and reading his paper. But we got on all right. He gave me one or two of his fags and he explained he'd joined in London. I often thought to chase him up afterwards, but his name was Brown, and looking for a bloke called Brown in London isn't really on. He was the only member of Workers' International League I ever came across in the army and within three days of seeing him I was posted abroad.

Italy: the Allies and the partisans

In 1945 I was sent over to Italy and arrived there just in time for the end of the war. One thing interesting about being posted abroad was the difference in the attitude of the officers. When you were in England training they were real snots. If they wanted you it would be, "That man there, here at the double!" When you went abroad and they were faced with the prospect that they might be walking in front of you and you would be there with a rifle and 50 rounds they suddenly remembered you had a name. Instead of, "That man there," it was, "Frank, here a minute, would you?" The difference in attitudes was quite pronounced.

Italy was a nice place to be. There was the odd occasion when some silly bugger shot at you, but that is the sort of thing that happens in war. Italy was a wonderful place. It took time to develop a taste for the wine. But what really impressed me—when we were in Rome, Udine and Trieste—were the partisans. They did a lot more fighting than British troops ever did. They would walk into bars that we were in, holding tommy guns with hand grenades around their belts. They would mingle with us and chat and there was a great deal of friendship and respect between the British troops and the partisans.[36] We shared a common hatred for the military police. They were brilliant—but having said that, I didn't have as much time as I'd have liked to fraternise in Italy. I was constantly on the move. At most I spent two or three weeks in one place before being moved on.

The attitudes of the junior officers to the resistance often reflected those of the men. There was a sort of mutual respect and you would hear, "I like these people." Among the higher command there was the idea that once Britain had done a deal with Field Marshall Badoglio—he was "one of us", a "a gentleman"—you could forget about the Italian fascists' use of poison gas in Ethiopia, and the partisans could be dismissed as nothing but "gangsters" and the British would carry out the wishes of Badoglio's government.[37] But these views meant nothing even to the junior officers.

In England the junior officers were nasty and snotty in the main because they were forced into being like that in training. Once we got abroad most were quite happy to throw all that out just the same as we were. It used to be that the army officers were the sons of the ruling class. My CO [commanding officer] when I was in Britain came from Davenport, from a millionaire family. He used to tell us how enjoyed serving as a boy soldier. We all knew he was a bloody liar. Daddy had bought him a commission in the Guards and when the war started and the Guards might be sent to where the fighting was, he got himself transferred to a training camp in Britain. But there simply were not enough scions of the ruling class to fill all the officers' posts so they had to pull in lower middle class people, like schoolteachers, and they had pretty much the same ambitions as the rest of the troops—to get back home and get out of it.

I heard a tale from my brother who was out in the Middle East with Montgomery.[38] When Montgomery was leaving to command the troops for the Normandy landings he had a parade. You'd have thought he was royalty, in the back of his car saluting all the troops, who were ordered to stand along the road and cheer. To show what a man of the people he was, he started throwing out packets of cigarettes. These were South African fags called "Springboks" and they were reputed to be made out of camel shit. I don't think that was right; it was a slander on the camel. Nobody would smoke them. We dried lemon leaves and rolled them and smoked them rather than these South African cigarettes. So when he threw them out of his car the men picked them up and threw them back at him. There was a general contempt for the upper ranks. Generally speaking, people hated Montgomery. But so many of the junior officers were what we would now consider working class. The best officer I ever had was a guy called George—that was his surname. He used to sneak out of the officers' mess when we were in Palestine and bring a crate of beer into our tent. He would have a drink with us and sit there till midnight drinking the booze he'd brought out of the officers' mess, because he couldn't stand the officers.

I got a feeling of revolution in the air—certainly in Italy, particularly in the north. There was that confidence on the part of the partisans. You felt they could do something. But it was difficult for an individual Trotskyist like myself to judge and our possibilities were so limited. You couldn't look round and assess the situation. You went where you were sent and you only got to look around particular areas. Quite often these weren't representative. Looking back, I think a socialist revolution could have developed in Italy, but for the role of the Communist Party. Even from my position, hardly speaking the language, it was possible to see the effect the Communist Party had on this militancy.[39]

Greece: British troops and the origins of the Civil War

At the beginning of 1946 I was posted to Greece. We got there just before the general election [of March 1946] which struck me as completely phony.[40] The British army was there buttressing a very right wing government against ELAS [the Greek People's Liberation Army] and EAM [the National Liberation Front] which had led the Greek people during the struggle against the Nazis. Contrary to what you might expect, it was one of the most enjoyable 12 months of my life. The people were extraordinarily friendly and when you got to know them it was surprising how many would tell us of their experiences with EAM or ELAS.

I remember having to sit in a jeep as a guard for this American woman who was the United Nations representative. She was supposed to be seeing that the election was run freely. She had a driver and myself as escort to protect her.[41] We were in Patras at the time and driving round and round, we couldn't see anybody. We used to drive her from one officers' mess to another. One day she said to me, "This must be an open and free election because there is no trouble and no noise and no shouting." I said, "You silly bugger, that is proof that it isn't a free election. If it was a free election there would be people shouting, people holding meetings. People would be scrapping and kids would be banging dustbin lids and banging each other's heads as well—that's a free election. When nobody moves, it's because they're too terrified." She wouldn't have that. She was convinced that the fact people weren't politically active was proof that they were active politically.

Fortunately, by being pretty useful at cricket, I managed to wangle a good job while I was in Patras. I was the only one capable of acting as a wicket keeper and on the wickets we played on it was a life-threatening position. The CO of our mob had been the pre-war captain of the Kent cricket team. He was an amateur, of course. You had to be a gentlemen to captain a team in those days. We had a practice match and I remember running him out when I was wicket keeper by cheating. Somebody threw the ball in to me and I was standing behind the wicket with my back obstructing the view of the umpire. I flicked the wicket with my toe and the bails went flying off before the ball was in my hands. All the umpire could see was the bails go up in the air and he could hear me appealing and see the bat was a couple of feet from the crease. So he gave the CO out. And the CO looked at me and said, "The umpire didn't see that, Henderson, but I did and I shall watch your career with interest." But actually what he did was arrange a good job for me because I was a good cricketer.

That job gave me the chance to meet people in ELAS. There was a referendum on whether the king should return. It was horrible. I'd have liked to have seen that American observer again. For a couple of weeks or more before the date of the plebiscite, anybody suspected of being opposed to the return of the king was pulled in and beaten up. Hundreds, possibly even thousands, were whipped up the mountainsides, barbed wire coiled round them and left there to rot until the plebiscite had finished. The Greek army and police did it—mainly the Greek police. We were only there for logistical support. The police were the same bastards who had been police during the German occupation. They had been police when the Italians were there. They were the police under Metaxas, the military dictator before the war, and they carried on happily as police under the British.[42] They were real swine.

Among the army it was a different proposition. The soldiers in the Greek army were still being called up. If they possibly could, they would duck out of doing anything against their own people. They certainly weren't completely trustworthy from the Greek or British point of view. The officer class, and there was a well defined officer class in the Greek army, were real bastards. They survived quite well acting on behalf of the Nazis during the war and the British and later the Americans after the war.

I managed to persuade my mates to commandeer this lorry and we loaded it up with supplies off a boat on the quayside. We managed to bluff our way in, load it up with stuff, take it into the hills and distribute it to these people who had been caged in. I think we overdid the soap when they would have much preferred food and chocolate. But we had to take what was on its way to the NAAFI.[43] We had to take what was going. I think that lorry load could have saved a few lives. Not long after, I was invited to a barbecue by the barman in a cafe just down the road. I went up the mountain and there was a detachment of ELAS. They had invited us more or less in response to what we'd done. It was great on the mountainside. They were roasting a sheep on a spit. I don't know what sort of sheep it was but it tasted good. And there we were, drinking retsina and dancing these Greek dances on the side of a mountain in our army boots. It takes some doing, but we managed it. They were great people.

We went from there to Salonika and I was transferred out of the Kensington regiment I was in at the time to the Engineers and to a workshop. We had 30 or 40 local Greek craftsmen working in this workshop and we got on well. When you got to know them, they would tell you about EAM and ELAS and it was great.

Then we were shifted back to Egypt and I was the last man to LEAP (Leave in Advance of Posting). That is what you got when you had been abroad for a certain amount of time, but not long enough to qualify for a home posting. I had a month's leave which turned into six weeks because they cocked up the boats when I was due to go back, so I had an extra couple of weeks out of it. I got back to Egypt thinking, "I'm just right for demob." But it didn't work out like that.

Duncan Hallas was just down the road.[44] He was in the canal zone at the same time I was and in one of the interviews with him in *Socialist Review* he told he how enjoyed swimming in the great lakes every day. I was there, a bit farther up the road, enjoying a swim in the same lakes every day. As far as I know, I never bumped into him. The annoying thing was they sent him home for demob and they sent me to bloody Palestine.

Palestine: the last days of British rule

I was only in Palestine for about three or four months.[45] I spent the time in Gaza, from which we hardly moved. We were not allowed out unless there were at least four of us, and we all had to carry tommy guns. Nobody went out. There was nothing actually to go out for. I remember Gaza as being pretty bad. Rafah was a small village. I look at it now on the television and realise that for every 100 people in the area then there must be about 15,000 now. Irgun killed a couple of blokes while we were there.[46] They were the terrorists.

While we were in Gaza there was a boatful of refugees—in the main, people who had survived the Holocaust and were being brought in a ship. We were brought out on alert, lined up along the coast and told to keep our eyes on that ship. If we saw any boats or anybody trying to swim to land from that ship we were supposed to shoot them. These were survivors from the Holocaust. They didn't particularly want to go to Palestine. The places they really wanted to go were the United States, Britain, Canada, Australia, New Zealand and a few to South Africa. Almost nobody among the survivors wanted to go to Palestine. This lot had sailed to America and been refused admission to the US. But people in America had subscribed to provde supplies to take them to Palestine. The US wouldn't accept them as refugees but it would finance shoving them into Palestine. That is when I got an idea that has stopped in my mind ever since, that the arguments over Palestine then were as much an attempt by the US to ease British imperialism out of a base in the Middle East and take it over, as about anything else. It was similar to how the Americans took over the struggle in Greece. Their designs were not just to be anti-Arab or anti-Greek, or even anti-Soviet. They were also anti-British. The only place in the world where Britain had any real imperial power left was in the Middle East. The US was in the process of pushing Britain out. I know when we were lined up with orders to shoot anybody who tried to get off that ship there was a unanimous, "Bugger off, we won't do it." And they pulled us out.

Demobilisation

Towards the end of the war there was unrest among the troops. Where troops were concentrated, and particularly where troops had seen a fair amount of service, was where the troubles were. For instance, it's worth understanding the position of people who were in group 26. You were given groups according to how old you were and how long you had been in. Group 26 consisted of people who had been called up for six months military training in the summer of 1939 and the war had started before they finished. So the six months had become six and a half years. At the end of the war the demobilisation of these people who had enlisted for six months was spread over another eight months. So these people who had been called up, say, in June 1939 were often still awaiting demob in January and February 1946. They tended to be a little irritated. They were old sweats who had seen a bit of activity and weren't going to be pushed around. What the army tried to do was leaven the bread. So anybody with any service was mixed up with a whole crowd of people who had only recently been called up. When I went to Greece there were probably 200 of us out of a battalion of 700 or 800 who had seen any sort of service and the others were fresh recruits. Even then we tended to be pushed out on detachments. It worked quite nicely for me in Greece because I was living in a hotel in the middle of town. I even had a bedside telephone. Unfortunately, the only number I knew was the talking clock. The only thing the troops really cared about was getting home.

I'm dubious about how many voted in the general election of 1945.[47] I think quite a few didn't get the papers. Having said that, feeling among the troops reflected the situation in Britain. People were pretty solidly Labour. As much as anything that meant being anti-Tory. There was a widespread feeling that "we're not going back to 1918. Our parents might have stood for it, but we're not standing for it this time." This attitude was the real reason for the birth of the welfare state. Troops used to sing the Red Flag but people used to sing that in boozers in Wolverhampton as well. The attitude among the troops was flavoured all the way through with the desire for demobilisation. The government could have made old age pensions £1,000 a week in Britain and no one would have believed it until they were sent back to Britain and demobbed. The question of demob coloured everybody's thinking. If someone was due for demob in a couple of weeks and it was only a question of waiting for the boat, they were really enthusiastic about what was happening in Britain. But if it looked as though they would have to wait any longer for demob then it was, "These bastards are just the same as the others." It occupied all the troops' minds: "The emergency's over. Why aren't we home?" That was how they judged every politician.

Troops demonstrated and mutinied about being sent home. They wouldn't accept the need for British troops in India as they had pre-war. People were saying, "Why should we be here telling them what to do? Or ruling them? We should be home." That was the feeling in Malaya and everywhere there were demonstrations by troops.

Chapter Three

Post-war Britain

Return home and the fate of British Trotskyism

The Revolutionary Communist Party disintegrated while I was still away.[1] It was fortunate for me. I passed the time away in Italy and Palestine while the infighting was going on in the RCP. The problem of trying to analyse the immediate post-war period was the basic cause of the split. We had argued the war would result in a catastrophic slump and this would sweep away social democracy, sweep away the Stalinists and allow genuine revolutionary parties to build. But, of course, at the end of the war we didn't get the catastrophic slump. Instead there was a worldwide boom in capitalism. There was only so far you could go on expecting the boom to end and crisis to follow. Gerry Healy could spend the next 40 years insisting the impending capitalist crisis was going to happen tomorrow and we were on the verge of a revolutionary situation, but it didn't rest very easily with day to day politics.[2]

As regards the Soviet occupation of Eastern Europe, I was conscious there were arguments going on among Trotskyists. I regarded the arguments as the kind you would expect in a time of change for a revolutionary party. People had to constantly to debate their position and attitude in a changing world. When I finally came home I found the organisation I was so proud of had disintegrated. It was a bit of a shock. Even worse, when I joined in with Healy's mob on the basis that they were the people I met up with, I found out—according to him—that people who I had supported almost to the point of hero-worshipping, people like Jock Haston, were supposed to be "traitors". It took some following.

The later development of the Workers' Revolutionary Party showed me that the guy who was its leading light, Gerry Healy, was nothing short of a gangster.

The reason I joined Gerry Healy's organisation, known as the "Club", was simply because they were the first people I met after I was demobbed.[3] I certainly didn't expect the disintegration of the Revolutionary Communist Party to reach the extent it did. I was dissatisfied with the Healy regime. But the Club was instrumental, with an assortment of CPers and Labour left wingers, in starting the Socialist Fellowship and producing the paper *Socialist Outlook*.[4] If not a brilliant paper, it did at least give us something to work round. It reduced our isolation. I was a Labour councillor at the time and trying to operate as a councillor inside the Labour Party was a little difficult as a 23 year old. But *Socialist Outlook* gave us a means of involving ourselves in political activity divorced from the social democratic politics of the Labour Party. It was tolerated, at least in the initial period. As a Labour councillor I could go to Labour Party meetings and sell *Socialist Outlook*.

The group split eventually. There was a clash between Healy and John Lawrence, who was the editor of the paper. Lawrence was a Pabloite and got kicked out, and Gerry was left ruling the roost.[5] Following the exit of Lawrence, the regime got tighter and tighter until in the end it was completely intolerable. When I supported a young recruit from Wolverhampton (in a row that came down to how much he could afford to pay) it led not to a formal expulsion or resignation from me, but to my being frozen out of the organisation—something that was quite tolerable for me.

The question of how we approached the Eastern European states and Russia came more and more to the fore in internal arguments. We had always argued, following Trotsky, that Russia was a "degenerated workers' state".[6] The argument was that the basis of a socialist society—nationalised industry—still existed there and all it needed was a democratic political revolution to remove the Stalinist ruling caste.

But how should we approach these new states in Eastern Europe?[7] At first there was general agreement that they remained capitalist states, even though they had governments imposed on them by the Red Army and the governments consisted of Stalinist stooges. The only exception was Yugoslavia. There was obviously a contradiction in accepting that the carbon copy was capitalist whereas the original was a workers' state.

There was also an argument about our attitude towards Tito and Yugoslavia.[8] I found this the last straw. Following the split between Tito and Stalin in 1948, the line of the Club was that Tito and the Yugoslav Communist Party, by remaining in Yugoslavia and engaging in partisan struggles against the Nazis, had maintained a measure of independence that allowed them to build socialism separately from the rest of the Eastern European states and Russia. So Tito became a socialist hero for the Trotskyists, at least the Healy Trotskyists, almost to the same degree that Stalin was a hero for Communist Parties across the world. I remember us selling little pamphlets produced by the Yugoslav Communist Party. Pablo and one half of the Fourth International argued we should become a part of the Yugoslav Communist Party and then extend it worldwide so that we would enter the Communist Parties and act as a left wing faction. Instead of the revolutionary party leading to workers' control and building a workers' state, Pablo argued the Communist Parties would be forced, whether they liked it or not, to lead the socialist revolution. That was a strange idea to almost every Trotskyist who had cut their teeth struggling against the counter-revolutionary role of Stalinism throughout the world. All of these arguments were reflected inside the RCP in Britain and the result was the party disintegrated.

The other argument was about the attitude towards the Labour Party. By one of those ironies of history, the people who argued we should remain an independent party outside the Labour Party in the end became the most loyal of Labour Party entrists— Ted Grant and co.[9] At that time Gerry Healy argued for work inside the Labour Party—and that is possibly what kept me. The Labour Party was then a mass party. It wasn't the party of the Bernie Ecclestones that it is today. I was a Labour councillor in a ward in Wolverhampton and we used to hold a meeting every fortnight in the Culwell Tavern and could guarantee 40 people there. What is more, we used to discuss politics. I was influential in that happening, but only to a certain extent. The fact was that critical arguments took place quite often at well attended ward meetings across the town.

In Wolverhampton we also had a young socialist organisation. This had started basically as a result of a few of us getting older. The age for finishing in the Labour League of Youth was 25. Most of us had done time in the army and come out at 21, 22, 23. In a couple of years, you were 25. So there was a bit of a vacuum because of conscription. The people you would normally be looking to recruit were being called up, pushed into the army or navy and sent all over the place. We wanted a little bit of continuity and that meant keeping people in until after they were 25. So we called ourselves the Young Socialists and acted independently rather than like the Labour League of Youth. We had some exhilarating political discussions and did quite a bit of work. It didn't necessarily happen the same way in youth organisations in other towns and cities. But there was lively political activity going on elsewhere centred on the Labour Party. So it was an area where you could work, talk and argue politics, and to divorce ourselves from that seemed to me to be ridiculous. It was much better to be embedded in the movement than to retreat from it. There was a glorious opportunity for us to talk to socialist workers. The problem we had when I first joined the Trotskyists, and throughout the war, was finding workers to talk to. Now we had a position where it was served up on a plate. To turn our backs on that to become an independent group of 200 seemed fanciful.

So the arguments that caused the split were about our attitude towards entry into the Labour Party, our attitude to the Eastern European states, and prospects for the economy—whether we were faced with a capitalist boom or a slump. For me as for so many others, there was a limit to how long we could wait for the slump to begin. Most of us were busy working and trying to organise workplaces. These different threads couldn't be held and there was nothing really to hold us together. The Communist Party had this genuine belief in Mother Russia and Joe Stalin. They had something to hold them together. After Trotsky died, there was nothing like that inside the Fourth International.

The result was that across the world the Fourth International disintegrated into little groups, each claiming to be the proper descendants of Trotsky. It struck me even at the time that the smaller the grouping, the more vociferous it was in proclaiming itself to be the one carrying forward the true traditions of Trotskyism. Most people ended up in the same position as myself, holding on to Trotskyist views, and the ideas of revolutionary socialism, but absorbed in the day to day struggle in industry, working inside the trade unions and so on. There was a whole reservoir of ex-Trotskyists like that with no strict relation to the Trotskyist movement, insofar as you could call it a movement.

Back to the track

After military service everybody was supposed to be guaranteed their former job for at least 12 months if it was still there. So I went back to where I'd been before. Although I got the full rate, I was still classed as an apprentice because I'd been called up before my time had finished. In the event, I only worked there nine or ten months because the aircraft industry was cutting back sharply after the war. But there was full employment and getting the sack didn't really mean that much. I went from there to the Austin because it paid well.[10] It involved travelling, but it was a highly paid job for manual work at the time. By the time I started, the workforce had just about become 100 percent trade unionist. Up until the war there had been vicious anti-union campaigns on the part of the management.

Some of the work practices were pre-war. They still had a crude way there. I remember it being a shock finding out that when they stopped or changed a model they just sacked all the workforce. That created a few arguments. People weren't going to accept that, particularly when they could see the gaffers trying to put people they didn't like on models coming to the end of the line.

This situation ended in 1953 when there was a big strike called the McHugh strike. One model—the A125—had finished and all the workers had been sacked. A guy called McHugh was the shop steward and for the first time at Longbridge, I think, there was a strike against the closure. It was a big strike and the settlement was that the company agreed to take back all the workers who had been sacked except the shop steward, McHugh. So all the vehicle builders, probably 40 percent of the workforce on the body side, went on strike and stopped out for 13 months. In the end, they were battered down and went back and McHugh didn't get his job back. But it was pretty much a pyrrhic victory for the management and after that they did not try the same procedure of sacking every-body. Although the union lost the strike in terms of getting the reinstatement of McHugh (who wasn't particularly bothered about coming back—he had already fixed himself up as an insurance salesman) it made the management think twice in future.

While that strike was going on, I was still working in Wolver-hampton at ICI, where I worked when I was demobbed. When I was sacked after about nine or ten months I went to work at the Austin and then skipped it in 1950 and went to work at Castle Bromwich for what was Fisher Ludlows, which became Pressed Steel Fisher and is now the Jaguar plant. I was made redundant there on the basis that I was single and went back to ICI from 1951 to 1953. I always remember the date of the coronation, 2 June 1953, because everybody else was given a day's holiday with pay and I got the sack. I tended to remember that. But it shows that jobs were available.[11] The jobs I mentioned were all plum jobs pay-ing good wages. If you got the sack and really wanted a job, you could get one anywhere you liked. A lot of the fear of the bosses was destroyed on that basis. It's what made working interesting in those days.

The situation with the bosses mirrored the way the officers in the army suddenly remembered your name and became extraordinarily polite and friendly when you were stuck there with live ammunition. The gaffers were anxious to avoid trouble so they talked to the shop stewards. As a shop steward at that time I could walk into the boss's office and say, "Now, look here, if you do this it's likely to cause all sorts of trouble, you know." And he'd say, "The last thing on earth we want is trouble. How can we get out of this?" It would save you looking for some sort of compromise. You could almost achieve what you wanted, at least step by step, just by a nod and wink and the threat of action rather than having to be involved in action.

Where there were strikes, as a rule it was at the start of a new job on a new model—over the manning levels or the piece rates for each operation.[12] The management tended to say, "This is as much as we can possibly afford. We cannot afford any more. The vehicle won't be economic if we pay what you are asking for." The shop steward would say, "The blokes won't stand for that and will walk out." The steward would report back to the blokes. They would say bugger this, put their coats on and walk off home, usually an hour or so before knocking off time, then come back in the next morning and the gaffer would say, "Now look here, let's start talking sensibly about this." It became part of the negotiation process, the short sharp strike that was as often as not budgeted for by the management and taken as being part of the procedure.

The official disputes procedure was laughable. It involved bringing in the local officials if the shop stewards couldn't deal with something. If the local officials couldn't deal with it, the regional officials came in; if the regional officials couldn't deal with it, the national officials appeared; and if the national officials couldn't deal with it, the confederation officials got involved. If the confederation officials couldn't deal with it then we would have a conference at York, where the employers' federation would discuss it. It would come back through these channels to the shopfloor, but by that time they had quite possibly finished making that model and started on another round. There was a standard joke, certainly at the Austin and at most of the factories where I worked, that if you wanted to shove a thing to one side and forget about it you would send it to York. "Sending it to York" meant it's a load of rubbish, chuck it away, bin it. That was widespread right up until the 1970s.

The Labour Party after the war

The austerity during the first post-war Labour government didn't damage the support for the Labour Party, which was solid. Although the Tories won the 1951 election, it was Labour that got a record number of votes.[13] Nye Bevan was a typical Labour leftist in action. He played a great part in pushing through the National Health Service, which captured everybody's imagination, although he made so many concessions to the consultants that it sowed the seeds of future trouble. Nevertheless, he had done this great thing. Many on the Labour left saw the choice as either rearmament or the health service and there was no contest, certainly at rank and file level. The Labour left then meant almost every individual member of the Labour Party. The Labour right were trade union officials and the cabinet or the parliamentary leadership. So it was easy to argue on the basis of a friendly approach to the Bevanites. I found no contradiction in arguing for revolutionary socialist politics at the same time as supporting the Bevanites against the leadership inside the Labour Party.

Councillor Henderson

Did I achieve things as a councillor? To sum it up: no. It was awful really. The councils then were a bit different to what they are now. The leading lights among Labour councillors then were people who had actually involved themselves in working class struggle, although they had settled down to old age and the comfort of full employment. For example, both the secretary and the chair of the Labour group on the council had been sacked as a result of the General Strike in 1926 and not been able to get a job until the war because they had been blacklisted. They had settled down as councillors circumspectly. They always listened to the officials a lot more than they deserved. But it was possible to argue for left wing views and what we were arguing wasn't whether we should sell off council houses, but whether we should buy more private homes to operate all the houses in the town as council houses, whether we should develop and extend municipal catering to make sure there were cafes that served cheap meals near the factories and so on. Quite advanced ideas were argued and they were argued as a matter of course—not what is happening now, where councils stoop to any sort of corrupt and dishonest manoeuvres to sell council homes rather than develop a housing policy that ensures people get the housing they need. What I found as a councillor in the end was that it was time consuming and, if you weren't careful, the minute details pulled you away from political involvement. It's a lot easier to go to a meeting and argue the toss for a couple of hours than to stand in the street or outside a public meeting and sell the paper. So many of those people who had a history of fighting and struggling up until the war found themselves regarding it as a great victory if they saw the housing manager and got someone who had come to see them a step up in the priorities for being rehoused. That was a great victory! It was a thing you had to do as a councillor, but when those little victories take the place of fighting for fundamental change in society, you've got something basically wrong.

Towards the end of the 1950s there was a new layer of councillors coming up completely different from the older councillors. These old councillors were right wing but they had been involved in struggles before and they tended to work democratically. So if you won a resolution in the Labour group, when it came to the council they would vote and argue in favour of the resolution despite their opposition at the group meeting. They would accept the party decision even if it was against their ideas. We won one or two like that. But this new generation who came through towards the end of the 50s were looking to make a career out of the business and they had no concept of loyalty to the Labour Party, to their colleagues or to the people who elected them.

I was on the council from 1952 to 1961. It was an awful long time. It cost me money to be a councillor. The expenses councillors claim now would put the fear of god in me. They claim thousands of pounds. When I went to a council meeting, I was allowed 15 shillings expenses and it took six or seven shillings to get there from work because I was working in Birmingham and had to knock off early to go the meeting. I know when I finished in 1961 it was costing me 50 bob a week to be a councillor.[14] Now they get £50,000 a year. The Labour Party has changed completely. You never get the meetings now that you used to. People were involved. I remember when I was elected in 1952. I had 40 people helping me every night for three weeks during the election campaign. We knocked on every door at least three times in the campaign—that is allowing for all the return trips for when people were out. We used to go around and hold meetings in the street. We'd knock on a door and ask to borrow a kitchen chair or a beer crate, stand on that on the pavement and have an open air meeting. We usually had about 10 or 12 who would stand around listening and arguing the toss with us. All that sort of thing has gone. There is no relationship between the councillors and the people they represent; there is no relationship between the councillors and any political ideas, any socialist ideas anyway.

As far as the Korean War went, in Wolverhampton—and I'm pretty sure this was reflected elsewhere—there was an acceptance of it among the older members of the party: reluctant, very reluctant, but an acceptance of it because they didn't believe a Labour leadership could be that bad and corrupt to support a war unless there were genuine reasons for it.[15] I found among the younger element, in particular, there was strong opposition to it. At every meeting whenever the chance came the arguments were raised against involvement. We used to win quite a few and get a resolution through from the constituency party to the national conference opposing intervention, opposing the Korean War. It had no effect whatsoever on the Labour leadership. But it was possible as a left winger to oppose the war and win the argument fairly easily within the local party right up to conference level which was dominated by the block vote held by people like Arthur Deacon from the T&G and Bill Carron from the AEU. These right wingers usually voted in defiance of their own union's conference decisions, exercising the vote "democratically" in favour of whatever the executive wanted.

When it came to war there was a brief moment when even the right wing in Wolverhampton agreed it was absolutely wrong. We had an open air meeting at the market place and right winger was quite happy to stand on the platform and denounce the Suez intervention.[16]

The smoke of Budapest reaches Wolverhampton

When it came to 1956 and the question of Hungary it was a bit different.[17] The right wing turned round and said, "We told you so.

What do you expect?" Among the left I found it easy to argue a Trotskyist line against the Russian intervention, calling for the removal of Russian troops from Hungary. The opposition to that came from the Communist Party, but in Wolverhampton it was pretty mute. We had an organisation called the Socialist Discussion Group and we produced a document on the invasion calling for the troops to get out and for support for the working class in Hungary and circulated it around—including to quite a few members of the Communist Party. Lo and behold, we were invited to go along and discuss it at their next branch meeting.

Two or three of us went. We found the leadership—George Masters, the secretary, Jeff Brotherton, the chairman and an old Stalinist diehard—trying their best to run the meeting so there wouldn't be a chance for us to speak, even though we'd been invited formally by a resolution obviously passed at the last meeting. But in the end the members of the Communist Party insisted we be given the chance to speak. We spent about an hour and a half arguing with them and having a debate. The official Stalinist leadership kept their mouths shut and we found quite an intelligent discussion coming from the rank and file of the party. We went away convinced we should build on this and circulated a newsletter. But they recovered from it and it faded out. One reason was that a socialist discussion group of a dozen people in Wolverhampton was not exactly a great pole of attraction. Nationally, that pole of attraction was the *New Reasoner*—a split from within the Communist Party eventually pulled by Gerry Healy into his Socialist Labour League. We came a very poor second locally to anything like that.[18] There were brief moments in the fifties of real pleasure— a break from the tedium.

Eyewitness to revolution in Algeria

From the time I was demobbed everybody accepted, inside the Labour Party anyway, that India should have its independence. There was never any argument about that. But the arguments we had about Malaya were quite bitter. Even lefties among the leadership who would vote against German rearmament were very cagey about the issue of the troops in Malaya.[19] Every battle had to be fought and every battle was a losing one really when it came to the imperialist wars. Everybody accepted—you could win the argument—that Kenya should be independent, that Malaya and Cyprus should be independent. You could always win that. What I found we couldn't win was the argument of the real diehards that before these countries got their independence Britain had to put them in their place. "Back the troops up first and when things are quiet we come out and let them carry on," they said. It seems a nonsensical argument.

I was involved to a degree in campaigning for Algerian independence.[20] To an extent, it was easy because it only involved the French. People would agree with you, but asking them to do anything— even if it only meant supporting a United Nations resolution criticising the French—was a different proposition. So although I could argue for Algerian independence and people were sympathetic, I can't say I made any real progress.

Algeria achieved independence in 1962. In 1963 there was a conference of worldwide supporters of the Algerian struggle at the university of Algiers on the theme "What are we going to do in the future?" I was invited and shook the hand of Ben Bella.[21] The only thing memorable about the conference for me was that one day I went on a deputation that toured the estate owned by Marcel Buffette, a French millionaire who had vineyards and fruit-growing plantations. We saw the farm that had been taken over by the workers. There was a lot of workers' control. The hotel where I stayed was run by a committee elected by people who worked in it. This farm was under the control of a committee elected by the workforce. It included a bottling plant, which bottled fruit juice, and the guy who was chairman of the committee was a bottle washer. I'm always pleased when I hear people say, "Do you think the country could be run by head cooks and bottle washers?" That bottle washer was more efficient than the people who had been in charge before him.

Included in the deputation was a member of the executive committee of the French Communist Party and a member of the executive committee of the Italian Communist Party who had served in the government—an experience he was happy to pass on at every opportunity. In the course of the questions, I asked this committee chairman, "How many people work in the bottling plant?" He said 40. So I said, "How does that compare to how many were employed under the French?" "They employed 20." So I said, "How many bottles do you bottle now compared to under the French?" And he said, "Just the same: 20,000 bottles."

These two very superior Communist Party executive members from France and Italy went up in the air.

"That's ridiculous!" They said: "Socialism is all about efficiency! If 20 people can bottle 20,000 bottles under the capitalists, ten people under socialism should be able to do 20,000 bottles."

This chairman couldn't read or write. He said, "I haven't the faintest idea about economics. But I know that 20,000 bottles under the French kept ten families alive and under us it keeps 20 families alive."

I thought, "Well, that guy knows more about Marxist economics than the experts from the French and Italian Communist Parties."

I was always a bit dubious about Ben Bella. He was a remarkably charming man. He reminded me very much of Nye Bevan. He had got a sort of aura about him—a really attractive personality. I've known Nye Bevan sit down at a table with a dozen people and they would sit with their mouths open listening to him. You had to be careful if you were one of them that your mouth wasn't open when you were listening. You had to constantly remind yourself, "Wait a minute, he is talking total rubbish." Bevan still made you feel great. Ben Bella was the same. I remember him saying he had learned his socialism in prison. I'm always a bit dubious about people who learn their socialism in prison. People have to learn their socialism through being involved in the class struggle rather than when scraping the mortar from the bricks of their cell. Ben Bella was a very weak socialist and a very strong nationalist, but he struck me as basically an honest man and I suppose that is why he was overthrown in the coup a year after.

While I was there I met Michel Pablo.[22] He was busy as an adviser to the Algerian government, working out a legislative programme to put workers' control of production in the constitution. He had great reams of paper laying out this scheme and he was still working on it when the coup took place, which put a stop to all that. A carbon copy of the same thing happened in Chile with the Pinochet coup. Pablo was busy there acting as an adviser to Allende.[23] It struck me then as not the sort of thing a great leader of the Fourth International should have been involved in—drafting constitutions when he should have been involved in struggle.

There is no doubt about it though—Algeria showed the possibilities of what could be achieved for workers with any sort of revolutionary leadership. From small hotels and street sweepers to the plantations and bottling plants, workers were taking control and running places efficiently and calmly. They hadn't the slightest problem whatsoever. The move towards workers' control was embedded in the slightest struggles. What struck me was what we missed through the absence of a revolutionary organisation, and I felt bitter that in my lifetime possibly the biggest reason why a world party of revolution had not been formed was due to the Stalinists who poisoned the ideas of socialism—ideas that had reached fruition in 1917.

Campaign for Nuclear Disarmament

It was impossible to live through the 1950s and 1960s without some sort of involvement in CND [the Campaign for Nuclear Disarmament].[24] I ducked out on the Aldermaston marches. But as my recollection goes, almost every other week there was a march somewhere or other for some aspect of CND. So by the end of the 1960s I was getting a bit tired of long country walks. Being in support of CND, being against the bomb, became that much old hat really. It was almost taken for granted. I remember one case at work where a shop steward had a section meeting calling for an overtime ban. "Ban the bomb" had become such a common slogan that at the close of the meeting he said, "That's all agreed then, carried unanimously, we ban the bomb." Everybody cheered and he was just getting down from the bench he was standing on when he suddenly realised, so he said, "And ban the bloody overtime too." "Ban the bomb" rolled off the lips in all sorts of circumstances. Once that word "ban" came out "the bomb" almost automatically followed.

I remember chairing a public meeting held by CND in the Civic Hall in Wolverhampton. As speakers we had Ben Levy, the playwright, and his wife Constance Cummings, who was a well known film star. The only time I got my photo in the *Express and Star* was when I chaired the meeting with celebrities like that and it filled the Civic Hall. I became involved in a minor argument from the chair. I thought I'd handled the meeting quite well, but Ben Levy said he had a son who was still quite young and when he was old enough to do military service he would leave it entirely to his son to make up his own mind. I said, "I've got a son in that situation. Yes, I'd leave him to make up his own mind, but I'd do everything in my power to argue with him not to join the forces." You ought not to say things like that at a public meeting because when the press quote you, all they quote is this joking aside and miss out all the content. CND acted throughout the later 50s and 60s as the background to all other activities, always there. When a shop steward said ban the bomb as well as the overtime he wasn't so wide of the general feeling.

Racism on the buses and Enoch's stomping ground

It was during the late 1950s that we first saw signs of racism in Wolverhampton and in Britain generally. The bus workers at West Brom went on strike demanding a stop to the employment of black people. I went down with one or two people from Wolverhampton to picket the strikers, distribute leaflets criticising the strike action. Some of them were even arguing for the sacking of existing black employees on the buses. To my horror, the bus workers in Wolverhampton went on strike just after. I was the vice-chairman of the council's transport committee at the time and arranged a meeting with the town clerk and the chief of the transport department and asked for the local union secretary and other union representatives to meet us. I had to chair the meeting as the employers' chief spokesman because the chairman was away at the time. I remember opening the discussion by saying how disgusted and hurt I was at the idea of the workers in Wolverhampton going on strike over a racist issue.

The secretary of the T&G said, "Mr Chairman, it's nothing to do with racism whatsoever; it's all to do with overtime. If the corporation employs these people, it'll drastically reduce the overtime worked by the rest of the staff—that's all.'

I said, "I'm even more disgusted at the thought that you've got a problem with your workers having to work overtime in order to get a living wage. I'm disgusted that you solve the problem by denying work to other working people. Instead of leading your men out on the racist grounds of excluding black workers, you should demand proper wages to put a stop to having to work overtime."

I felt a bumping in my ribs when I was saying this. The town clerk put his hand over his mouth and whispered in my ear, "Chairman, it's not usually the position of the leader of the employers' side to recommend strike action."

The meeting finished, talks completely broke down. While the dispute was on there was supposed to be no negotiation. I wasn't happy with that. I know that is the normal negotiating position. But what I did was find the boozer where the strikers drank—the Barley Mow down the bottom of Stafford Street. So I went there and I found I got a reasonable reception. In a short space of time the strike was resolved in so far as the blokes went back and we did employ black workers. But it was a bit of a shaker for me, something I never dreamed would happen until it hit us.

Racism was one of the reasons why our local Labour MP got deselected.[25] He was recognised as a left winger and was a member of every workingmen's club in his constituency (that was taken for granted), including one, North Road Club—which, believe it or not, was in North Road. The chairman of the committee of the club was a Labour councillor and there were two other Labour councillors on the committee, and they expelled the MP from the club because he had publicly attacked workingmen's clubs for not accepting black members. They pursued a witch-hunt against him in the Labour Party which resulted in his deselection. As it happened, he died before the 1964 election anyway. But the Labour councillor who was chairman of the North Road Club had actually attended an organising meeting for the National Front. When we tackled him about it, he said, "Yes, of course, I went and quite a few of us went because the National Front isn't a political organisation, so there is no reason why we can't be Labour councillors and support the National Front." In the end the worst of the racists were frozen out, but it's an indication of the attitude some of these Johnny come lately Labourites were guilty of.

There were campaigns against racism. I wouldn't say there were a great many. It wasn't a weekly occurrence or anything like that. We did have quite a series of marches, meetings and so on. I remember we picketed one pub that was refusing to serve black people. That was fairly easy. The brewers didn't mind getting rid of one manager and employing another. Whether the policy changed is a different thing. The campaign against racism really took off in Wolverhampton strongly because we had got Enoch Powell.[26] Things tended to merge—the arguments against racism, arguments against Enoch Powell and the general anti-Tory arguments.

When it came to specifically anti-racist struggles of any broad nature, these really began in the 1970s. When I joined the International Socialists, I think the first duty they imposed on me—almost a week after I'd joined—was to speak at an anti-racist public meeting on the steps of Saint Peter's Church, facing what was then the market place and is now the Civic Centre.[27] We had a meeting there because Colin Jordan, who was a Nazi leader and who came from Coventry, planned to organise a parade round Wolverhampton. We organised a counter-parade and marched the route. Jordan couldn't actually get anybody to go on his parade and we had a big meeting in the square afterwards and then moved to the Town Hall, where he was supposed to be marching. No one turned up for his march, except Jordan and presumably a driver. He had a big Land Rover and he was standing in the back as though he was Hitler reviewing the troops.

One of our members got pinched for spitting as the Land Rover went past and he was rushed off to the nick. After things had quietened down, I was deputed to go to the police station and get him out. I was picked on the basis of being an ex-councillor. I had a respectable background, on top of which I was wearing a tie, so therefore I should do it. I went down there and it didn't make much difference being an ex-councillor or wearing a tie. Two hours later when I got out, I discovered that he had been released after a few minutes. They had released him but hadn't told me and subjected me to all sorts of harassment and abuse including threats to lock me up as well while I was trying to negotiate bail terms. But it was a little later, during the 1970s, that the real struggle against the Nazis began.

Shop Stewards in the 1950s and 1960s

The idea of "I'm alright Jack", portrayed in the film of the same name, was not new. During the war they portrayed being a shop steward almost as being a Nazi agent or being a trade unionist as a crime. It simply bore no relation to what people thought. I can't understand how people bothered to watch *I'm Alright Jack*.[28] It was taken a bit farther and a bit nastier than the Gracie Fields' pictures before the war, when she was always the daughter of a mill worker and the mill was closed because they were on hard times but she fell in love with the gaffer's son who was always nice, handsome and caring. In the end they all finished up linking arms, gaffers and people, singing "Sing as we go" or what have you—all nonsense.[29] In the late 1950s there was still the beautiful daughter and the handsome son, but it was set against a different background. Instead of it being one of unemployment—the work-shy bastards leaning against the gates outside the pits or the mills—workers in these films were now leaning against packing crates or what have you inside the plant. Films still portrayed workers as work-shy idle bastards. The only time that didn't apply was during the war. Young people in the 1930s were always attacked for being work-shy layabouts, lacking in respect for their elders and betters, organising themselves into gangs of thugs and thieves. No sooner was war declared than these thugs and thieves and layabouts became our boys willing to give up their lives for king and country.

At the end of the war, they became a gang of layabouts and thugs again. So what? We paid no attention whatsoever.

The film *The Angry Silence* was about scabbing. Whenever I'm faced with a scab I have to do one of two things: ignore him or spit.[30] Nobody's going to tell me that I'm committing a great sin by refusing to speak to a scab when he has tried to take away my livelihood by breaking up the union organisation I'm a member of. I don't think anybody took any notice of the film apart from a few reviewers in a few papers. I'm sure the *Daily Mail* was very fond of *I'm Alright Jack* and approved of *The Angry Silence* and its portrayal of workers. But then the *Daily Mail* had supported the Blackshirts.

We were on strike when the company was building the new West Works and we had got a picket up on the gate. Building workers had been sent into work on the back of these lorries by the gaffers. They came and let us know they weren't prepared to cross a picket line, but there had to be somebody there. We got on very well with them. We had quite a crew there. But the *Evening Mail* had a picture of us pickets standing in front of some of the building and a headline across the front page was "INTIMIDATION". In fact the building workers were bringing us cups of coffee from the cafe down the road, wishing us all the best.

Before the 1970s it was the Communist Party that pushed for a shop stewards' movement. There were broad lefts in the unions, but the real organisation, the real link, was the Communist Party, even where it did not have the members. It operated through the membership of branch committees, trades councils and quite often in the lower reaches of the union bureaucracy. In the electricians' union CP members were even in the top ranks of the union bureaucracy. This helped the party to forge together some sort of movement. We had the Engineering and Allied Trades Shop Stewards Organisation that had taken off before the war, but had disgraced itself pretty abominably during the war and never recovered its influence. Nevertheless, it helped to establish an unofficial organisation across the unions. There was an "official unofficial" organisation that was dominated by the Communist Party—which became the Liaison Committee for the Defence of Trade Unions

(LCDTU). Really, by the time it formed as an official structure the LCTDU was only codifying what had been happening.[31] By the time the CP got round to organising the LCTDU, its power was beginning to wane in the plants. Insofar as a movement was concerned, it was an organisation of the Communist Party rather than a genuine shop stewards' organisation.

Rank and file militancy without politics

Among shopfloor workers, it was of very little account whether a shop steward was a member of the Communist Party, CND, conservative or what have you. I remember one of the most militant shop stewards we had in the West Works at Longbridge was a Tory and he was quite a good fighter. As long as it was a purely sectional demand, as long as it benefited him and his little section, he didn't mind who he trod on, who he kicked about by going on strike. He expressed it in terms of, "Look after number one first, and look after my section second because I'll always get a kickback from that." Generally speaking, people ignored the outside politics of the shop steward. What they wanted was somebody who could represent them properly on the job. For most of the 50s and 60s at Longbridge nobody gave a damn who was on the works committee and whether the works committee functioned. At best, they saw the role of the works committee as one organising support for them if they were in dispute and if they wanted the support. Otherwise they would say, "What's it got to do with them?"

This attitude was even more pronounced towards the officials. I remember in 1958 when the management told us we had to get rid of our toolboxes. We used to line along the track, all with our toolboxes, using them for seats and god knows what as well as having tools in them. The management decided this was untidy and we had to use lockers in designated areas. They were going to throw all these toolboxes out. Our leading steward said, "Don't you dare." The next thing we know, they're using a stacker truck to get rid of the toolboxes. So we called a mass meeting and recommended strike action. I remember when the mass meeting was called in the car park. One of my jobs as a steward was to go and whip all the stragglers in to get them to the meeting. Contrary to the propaganda of the time, what we wanted at mass meetings was everybody there. It wasn't a select group of people who organised and told people what to do. Rather you had everyone there. I was a whipper-in and as I was making my way into the meeting I was stopped by one of the local managers who said, "Will you tell Bill ('Burglar Bill' Taylor was the leading steward) that the general secretary's here to see him".[32]

"I'll tell him".

When I got to the meeting, I wormed my way to the platform and said, "Bill, I've just had a message that the general secretary's here to speak to you." He said, "What the bloody hell's it got to do with him? Tell him I'll talk to him after, when I've got time."

And that was the message I relayed back. The idea of what's it got to do with him was commonplace. If there was a problem to be dealt with, he was going to deal with it, and whether his members were going on strike or not, they were going to deal with it. If they wanted the officials in, they would ask for them—otherwise keep out. That was the general attitude. I wouldn't mind betting that in the 1950s there wasn't one trade unionist in a hundred, or one in ten anyway, who knew the name of the general secretary of their union, because the people in these positions were basically irrelevant to the whole process. They were only relevant in terms of maintaining the fiction inside the Labour Party that the unions were backing the party leaders, because the top officials of the union backed the Labour right wing at conferences. In terms of the shopfloor, they meant nothing.

What the Labour government's *In Place of Strife* (1969) did was focus the minds of shop stewards a bit—certainly among the Communist Party.[33] That is when the Communist Party started calling meetings and conferences, where they would go through the motions of opposing wage restraint and any limitation on union organisation or membership. As far as the shopfloor was concerned, *In Place of Strife* had an effect, but not a dramatic one.

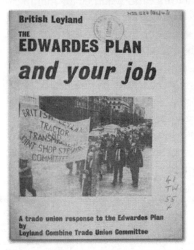

Clockwise from top left: *Socialist Appeal*, the paper of the
Workers' International League; *Socialist Worker* celebrates the
victory at Saltley Gates, 1972; *Carworker*, the rank and file
newspaper from the 1970s; the pamphlet that got Derek
Robinson sacked from Longbridge.

CHAPTER FOUR

The upturn and retreat

The British upturn: industry in the early 1970s

The election of Tory prime minister Ted Heath in 1970 changed the situation completely.[1] By the time Heath introduced the Industrial Relations Act in 1971, people were becoming politicised.[2] Industry was on the front page of the newspapers every day and you couldn't be a shop steward in Longbridge without being demonised in the press. People were beginning to look outside their own workplace. When the unions called a one-day strike in 1971 people followed it without any messing. They were hoping that would see off the attacks and things would go back to normal. But things never did, of course.

Saltley Gates and the miners' victories

There was jubilation at the miners' strikes of 1972 and 1974—particularly the 1972 strike.[3] When we had the three-day working week imposed by Heath, management tried to involve the unions as much as possible in governing it.[4] Management wanted a three-day week that suited their order books, with a full working week if they thought they could maintain it and make profits. So they tried as much as they could to involve the shop stewards in organising the three-day week, not to operate it fairly but as management wanted it. In the end, if you wanted to work a three-day week, that was what you worked and anybody who wanted to work more worked more. The whole thing was farcical. I remember one bloke saying, "It's great, this three-day week. I'm working six days and getting paid overtime for 'em."

We were affected by power cuts when the power workers went on strike, but not to the extent of other factories. Longbridge had its own power plant and the national grid supply was only for pilot lighting in case the firm's supply broke down. We were often held up, not by a lack of lighting in our place, but because power cuts in other places stopped supplies coming—which was fine because we still had light to play cards. There were power cuts at Christmas 1973 and I remember going to see my brother who lived in Longbridge. There were lights shining all round the Longbridge works and he was sitting in his house by candlelight. We absconded to the pub, which was lit by candles, and they couldn't serve any draught beer because they needed electricity for the pumps. So we had to drink bottled beer all over Christmas. Apart from the awful bind of having to drink bottled beer instead of draught beer, the disputes went quite well.

The victories in the early 1970s came one after another. Everybody really enjoyed themselves. Everyone would join a day's strike against the Industrial Relations Act, no problem at all. Everybody was overjoyed by the miners and when Saltley Gates closed everybody though how great it was.[5] The victories sent a tremor through you. Everybody felt great about it.

I was at Satley Gates, but there were only one or two from Longbridge. It was the East Birmingham District of the AEUW[6] that called the strike in support of the miners and they moved from East Birmingham to Saltley. Longbridge was under the West District Committee, which ignored Arthur Scargill's call to action. That included people like Dick Etheridge and Derek Robinson, the convenor and deputy at Longbridge. It didn't alter the fact that everybody was overjoyed and would have gone down, there is no doubt about it. People spent more time with the track stopped talking about the dispute as it was going on than they did doing any work.

I just stood at a gate at Saltley. There were so many there. I've heard all the different figures and I don't know how many. I know it was a great crowd. I couldn't get up to the front. I couldn't get out to the back. I was just stuck there until everybody dispersed. I spoke to Arthur Harper, who was president of the East District of the AEUW. He told me how it happened. Arthur reckoned there were 20,000 there; the cops reckoned 10,000. I thought it was more than 20,000. It depends who is standing on your feet at these things. The deputy chief constable of Birmingham who was in charge of the police operation got hold of Arthur and said, "Arthur, I've only got a couple of hundred police and you've got 10,000 men here on strike. You've got the whip hand today but remember this, I can have 20,000 policemen here tomorrow."

Arthur said, "Remember this, Deputy Chief Constable, you get 20,000 police here tomorrow, I'll get 200,000 pickets." He said the deputy police constable went white. That was probably an exaggeration. The whole thing might be an exaggeration, Arthur was prone to that but the fact that he could tell that sort of story immediately after demonstrated the mood. I'm sure Arthur would have had a go for his 200,000 men and, if it had been organised, I think they would have got 200,000 from the Birmingham area—a lot more easily than the Deputy Chief Constable would have got 20,000 coppers. The gates closed on the basis that the police were hopelessly outnumbered. If Arthur had said, "Let's storm them gates…", that would have been it. Everybody was buoyant. Having said that, there was a certain sense of superiority on the part of a lot of trade unionists in Birmingham. They were all pretty highly paid and were sympathetic towards these miners who had let their wages slip down the league table. But part of their attitude used to be, "Oh, you miners can't really win this on your own, but we'll give you a lift anytime you like, boys." It was patronising in a way but it made a terrific breakthrough.

The one blot on the period was the way the union let management introduce measured day work.[7] There were mass meetings on the day in November when the government was expected to announce a wage freeze. The works' committee said, "If we accept measured day work, we'll get this rise immediately, but if we don't make a decision before 3 o'clock when the minister makes his announcement, there'll be no wage increase." There was a fairly sizeable wage increase attached to acceptance. It's worth a sprat to catch a mackerel. The works committee generally recommended acceptance of measured day work.

Joining the International Socialists[8]

As far as I can recall, May '68 didn't create much of a ripple in Longbridge.[9] The way I recall it now, we were more concerned with Barbara Castle at the Ministry of Labour than things as far away from Longbridge as Paris—even as far away from Longbridge as Birmingham University. That changed later. I found myself invited quite often to speak at meetings in the university. I began to think I was a student at one time. I remember going to one typical student meeting. We were in this room, half dark, with students sprawling on the floor. Where students weren't strewn over the floor it was knee deep in beer cans. There was a blue haze of smoke from these French cigarettes whose name I still can't pronounce. I remember often having to speak to meetings like that and, when the queen came to visit Birmingham University, opening some faculty or something, I was invited to speak to some anti-royalist meeting. They told me I needed to be there for 12.30 so I drove there and got there at 12.30, only to find the queen was on the point of leaving. They had given me the time the visit finished rather than the start of the meeting. That was par for the course. Anyway, I'd been working nights so I thought I'd get home after calling in at the bookshop in the middle of Birmingham. I started to drive out of the university and found myself being escorted by a couple of motorcycle cops. I had to follow the queen's procession all the way into Birmingham. I stuck rigidly to the speed limit and there were all these cops trying to wave me on, with kids waving union jacks at me. It wasn't until we got to the island at Smallbrook Ringway that I turned off for the bookshop, and left the coppers. That was typical of the students: get everything organised but mess up the finish and the start. Having said that, the majority on the student committee were from the International Marxist Group not the International Socialists, so I can be a bit sectarian about it.

Vietnam had an impact. I don't think I found anyone who supported the Vietnam War. People generally accepted the war was wrong, that the yanks should be out, and most were prepared to go along with the slogan "Victory to the Vietcong". In terms of translating that into action, I didn't see much evidence of it at Longbridge. For somebody like me, the Tet Offensive was a little holiday in my heart.[10] You couldn't call the Tet Offensive a victory except in one respect, in proving to the yanks they couldn't win. But that was my own feeling of jubilation. It was possible to hold meetings on the war in pubs outside the plant where you would get a reasonable attendance and discussion. But as things developed after 1968, with many other issues directly involving Longbridge, Vietnam tended to be pushed to one side inside the plant.

Longbridge, being the size it was, became a magnet for all sorts of people who wanted to give out leaflets or sell pamphlets. Quite regularly the Jehovah's Witnesses would even present leaflets outside the plant. I managed to avoid most leaflets, but I was always a sucker for any paper being sold outside. Every weirdo sect tended to sell papers outside at some time or other. But they never used to last long. There would be a burst for a few weeks and then people would disappear.

Around 1970-71 *Socialist Worker* began to be sold outside the plant. I thought it was quite a good paper and after I'd been buying it for a time I thought I ought to do a little more than pay my tuppence as I went in. So I started giving half a crown for the paper. Well, the paper was tuppence—half a crown was 12 and a half papers. It would be equivalent to somebody giving a tenner for a paper now. After I'd done this for a couple of months or so, it struck somebody that if somebody's prepared to pay ten times what the paper was worth we ought to be talking to him really. So the sellers started to try to talk to me, but it was not that easy. I was quite skilled at talking to people when I wanted to talk to them rather than the other way around.

There was a book advertised in *Socialist Worker* by Tony Cliff: *The Employers' Offensive: Productivity Deals and How to Fight Them* (1970).[11] Cliff always insisted he didn't write it, but his name was on the cover.[12] The book cost six shillings. I thought, I will read it, because I could see signs of an employers' offensive beginning, and I wanted to see what *Socialist Worker* had to say about it. So I wrote my name and address on a bit of paper. The following Thursday night as I was going into work I gave the paper seller this strip of paper with my name and address, plus the six bob for the *Employers' Offensive*. I thought that might be a bit of a test for them. If I didn't hear any more, somebody had walloped my six bob and they were a bunch of thieving bastards. They might send the book to me, in which case they're not really serious. Or, if they are serious, the heavy mob would bring the book in person and talk the hind legs off me.

The following Sunday afternoon Paul Holborow and Dave Hughes came to see me and we spent several hours arguing the toss, mainly on the class nature of Russia. I'd been brought up to view Russia as a workers' state and from what I'd seen of people who believed in state capitalism I wasn't over-impressed until that time. I could remember what had happened to James Burnham, so I was instinctively hostile.[13] But I couldn't find anything in the paper really worth arguing about. So after a few hours arguing I agreed I'd join on condition that I could argue the toss over the workers' state in Russia whenever the situation genuinely arose in discussion inside the party. I agreed on my part that I wouldn't artificially raise the question of the workers' state.

They came round to see me the following Sunday, by which time I'd got a bit of a wind up. When they greeted me, I said, "I've changed my mind. I don't think I will join. The difference is too big." So we went through it all again. In the end the result was the same. I found myself recommended for membership. That might look a queer setup today. When you joined then you were recommended for membership and invited to a meeting. Paul Holborow had to attend the next meeting of the International Socialists in Wolverhampton and tell them about this contact he had who he wanted to recommend for membership, and the members agreed I should be invited to the next meeting. So he invited me along and introduced me. To my disgust, he introduced me as a veteran of the movement—and there was me thinking I was part of the socialist youth!

Anyway, I was accepted as a member and thought, "Well, that's enough. I'll take it easy for a start." But before the meeting finished, I was lumbered with a job as literature secretary. I didn't come away from the meeting totally impressed. It seemed to me a bit elitist, this idea of reporting there was someone you'd like the branch to meet when they should be welcoming anybody with open arms. If they didn't like the way someone operated they could always kick them out later. It was nonsense. What we want is as many people as possible. We can sort out the wheat from the chaff in the process of activity. They sorted the wheat from the chaff with me because the next Saturday I had to speak at the meeting following the march against Colin Jordan [see chapter three] and that was Cup Final day. It was the first time I'd ever missed a Cup Final and it really tested me, but I was there instead of waiting for the kick off. Looking back, the organisation had some weird ideas at the time. Well, I think they are weird.

The Birmingham pub bombings, 19 November 1974

When it came to the Birmingham pub bombings, I've never been so scared in all my life.[14] When we went to work the day after, most of us didn't know anything about them. News was only just circulating by word of mouth. Nobody was working. Tracks weren't working. Everybody was going round asking what had happened. During the course of the day all sorts of vile anti-Irish things came out: really poisonous stuff. A head of steam was building for a demonstration—a real pogrom—against anyone Irish. I spent all morning going round arguing against this with everybody I could find. I knew a march had been planned around the plant with a demonstration outside what they called the Kremlin, the top administration block.

There was a shop stewards' meeting on the west side (the body side, where I was) probably representing about 2,500 workers. Everyone was baying against the Irish, you know: "Kick all the Irish bastards out", "We ain't working with these Irish sods",

"Sack 'em all—they're killers." We found out during the course of the morning that one of the kids caught in the explosion, who had both his legs blown off, worked in our place. He was a kid of 18 or 19 and everyone was inflamed.

People were raging mad at the shop stewards' meeting. It was a lynchmob sort of atmosphere. I thought, "I've got to do it. I've got to put the blame for this on British imperialism and call for the withdrawal of British troops." But I was scared stiff. "If I keep my mouth shut," I thought, "after a week or so it will all fade out and people will have forgotten it." In the end, I got up and argued against the witch-hunting, against any pogrom. I said the people responsible for the bombing were the people responsible for all the trouble in Northern Ireland and that was the British imperialists, and the only way the problems of Ireland could be solved was by destroying the influence of British imperialism on the future of Ireland and that meant the withdrawal of British troops from Ireland. And I sat down shivering, ringing wet with sweat and expecting a real onslaught. Instead what I'd said was more or less dismissed as, "Well, that's Frank on again."

The meeting finished with an agreement to go on the march. I don't think I would have had the nerve under normal circumstances to get up and argue the way I did in a meeting of that sort if I hadn't been a member of the IS. That is the advantage of being in a party. It gives you a bit of backbone when things are tough. I think, without being a member of the International Socialists, what I would have done was sit there, keep my thoughts to myself and let the whole thing wash away. But I noticed, possibly as a result of what I'd said, that a lot of banners saying "Sack all the Irish bastards", "Kill the Irish bastards", and slogans like that were chucked on the floor and people were walking over them. From the end where I'd spoke people were carrying banners saying, "Bring our boys home". Now, "Bring our boys home" is a long way from a slogan like "Troops out now" but it's a bigger distance from "Hang all Irish bastards". I felt, possibly for the first time in my life, a little pride in myself for doing something. It was a lesson in the value of being a party member that has stuck with me ever since.

There were a couple of Irish stewards, one of whom was a member of IS, and the other used to come along to our *Carworker* meetings.[15] They were tougher than me. They went and argued it out with Irish accents. At least I'd got a Midlands accent and a background of 20-odd years working with these people. As a Brummie, I was scared stiff, yet these two comrades stopped there and argued the toss. I think it was more them than anything I did. The very fact of them arguing forced people to face up to the situation. Sack somebody, hang somebody, meant hang this bloke, somebody they elected as a steward. It made people think twice and draw back from the whole murderous, witch-hunting atmosphere. Our members did us proud.

Economic crisis and the effort to break shopfloor organisation

Two major things happened in the 1970s. There was a rapid increase in the price of oil which started the cost of living spiralling, and it signalled that public workers' wages had slipped far behind those in the private sector and they had to do something about it. I remember in the 1950s, in 1952 I think, I was offered a job as a teacher in West Brom at a technical college. It would have meant a six-month training course and I turned it down because I couldn't afford the loss of wages. Working in the factory was that much better paid than working as a teacher. But in the early 1970s people working in public services—teachers, nurses and, fundamentally, the miners started to fight for increases in their wages—to bring their wages at least to something comparable with private industry.

I remember the nurses put in a national claim, I think it was in 1971, and we went on strike for a day in their support. It wasn't just a gang of militants at Longbridge involved—hundreds of thousands of workers across the country went on strike in support of the demand of an increase in wages for the nurses. Workers were winning good claims in the public sector at the time. But in the private sector the boom was coming to an end. With the increase in the oil price and the inflation that went with it, the economy was sinking into recession.

Measured day work

The pressure on wages and conditions in private industry showed up at Longbridge in the struggle over "measured day work".[16] Under this scheme, everybody would work for the standard wage rather than piece rates. People were assessed into five grades according to their job description and the wage rate for those grades was negotiated at a top level of management in the plant—if these failed, then negotiations would take place at an even higher level outside the plant. The union officials took away the individual shop stewards' heavy involvement in the arguments about wages and bonuses that had gone on beforehand. It was an attempt to cut down shopfloor representation and the role of shop stewards.

The measured day work agreement was forced through by union officials from the outside. The works committee leadership inside the plant—basically dominated by the Communist Party—gave way to the officials, but the company had to pay a pretty high price. It took several years before the management clawed back the extra money they had to pay out in order to introduce this system. However, it went a long way to destroying the link between the shop steward and the workers he represented—no longer was the shop steward involved in negotiating the most important issues affecting the workers in a section. The shop steward became more and more a messenger boy rather than a leader because he had to take any problem to the works committee, which then went through procedures totally disconnected from the steward. In the end, shop stewards either got fed up and wouldn't take the job or just accepted it and slid into looking for a cushy number rather than involving the men they worked with. Before the system was introduced there was no way a shop steward would give way on a question of piecework if the blokes had told him what they wanted. It was no good a steward giving way and accepting something else. He had to go straight back on that job. He was working under the same conditions and for the same wages. So there was nothing to be gained. But once management had the measured day work system and later, when they included what they called "participation", it meant once there was a problem they took the steward away from his job sometimes for days on end. When he walked back in, he'd had a good scrounge, even if nothing had changed for the men he represented. So there was a weakening of the link between the shop stewards and their section, and the stewards came to be looked at in many cases as representatives of the officials rather than leaders or representatives of the section they worked in.

Carworker: a rank and file paper

A principal aspect of International Socialist policy that was distinctive was the focus on developing the strength of the rank and file. We were always careful about offering support to the full time officials, especially the national full-timers. We thought very much along the lines of the Clyde Workers' Committee during the First World War. It said, "We were willing to back the officials in so far as they fight for the workers' interests, but when the officials move from that we will work independently of them." The emphasis on rank and file activity was displayed in everything we did and said, but in particular in the attempt to get rank and file newspapers off the ground.

The IS began to produce up to 13 rank and file papers including Carworker.[17] Roger Cox edited it and carried the bulk of the work, assisted by people like Dave Lyddon who was working at Cowley and Gerry Jones from Coventry who was working at Rootes, which is now the Renault place, with myself at Longbridge, alongside quite a few others. We found we could sell Carworker pretty well to start with. The problem towards the end of its career, later in the 1970s when there had been a sharp drop in militancy, was that the sales of Carworker began to coincide with sales of Socialist Worker, so it lost its impact as a rank and file paper. It was only kept together by the involvement of a select few, and once a rank and file paper is kept together by a few it's not functioning as a rank and file paper. We had really needed Carworker up there and functioning at the beginning of 1970 instead of 1973. If we had

had *Carworker* in 1970, it would have been a different thing. But we would have needed a membership of 3,000 or 4,000 to do that instead of a membership of 1,000. It was a question of the organisation being too small to take on effectively the big problems that came. I put the blame for the organisation being small at the time on the old Communist Party. The Stalinists destroyed the possibility of serious political or industrial work among a majority of militants for a couple of generations. We had to start from scratch when we should have been starting from the springboard of a good solid organisation.

The Rank and File Movement and Longbridge factory branch

We had a factory branch of the International Socialists at Longbridge. I think we were the last factory branch to survive. We had a branch that at its best had 22 to 23 people. Almost by definition, if you're in a factory branch, you're active. You can't walk away from a meeting and go to bed. You're working with people. We found it relatively easy to sell the paper. We reached the peak of our influence in 1974 when the negotiation over the wage increase was dragging on and on.

The new style of negotiation was in effect as we moved to measured day work. The works committee, plus a negotiating committee of shop stewards drawn from across the plant, moved away day after day to a plush hotel in Worcestershire, closeted with management discussing an agreement clause by clause. It went on endlessly week after week. So we put in a double-sided A4 bulletin describing where the negotiations had got to, calling for a halt and for the negotiators to come and report back to the shopfloor in order for us to develop a bit of muscle before they went in with management again.

That really set things alight. Sections started going on strike in support of our demands. That is when Derek Robinson first threatened to throttle me. But the negotiators had to come back to the plant, report to mass meetings and explain what they were doing. It had quite an impact. But afterwards things started to slide—a reflection of the general loss of militancy rather than active disagreements with *Carworker*. One problem was that the branch was full of young people and quite a few got disheartened when the level of militancy dropped sharply towards the end of the 1970s. We found them giving up the job to work somewhere else. In the first years of the 1970s we had been organising rapidly, but in the last years of the decade we were losing that. The situation shifted completely.

When it came to the social contract, people accepted our argument that it was a "social con-trick".[18] I'm pretty sure the works committee accepted the con-trick position merely to try to reduce the influence of the International Socialists and *Carworker*. They called a conference in Birmingham Town Hall supposedly to organise resistance to the social contract. But at the conference the works committee—the Communist Party, in particular—had a change of heart and recommended we support the social contract and call on the Labour government to negotiate with responsible people like Derek Robinson. That was the role the CP tended to play. They would take the first steps of militancy and then divert everything away from activity. Having said that, I don't want to talk about the Communist Party as though it was just a complete monolith. A lot of Communist rank and file members paid their party dues, maybe went to party meetings and supported the Communist Party's political position in general terms but when it came to their individual sections they would pursue their sectional needs. Some of them would support the most outrageous class collaboration advocated by the CP as long as it was a way removed from them, but on issues near to them they were quite militant workers. A common result was that the Communist Party did just enough to drive its members out of political and even trade union activity when these people should have been the core of a fight against the bosses.

We participate, they profit

The biggest blow to shopfloor power in British Leyland was the establishment of the so-called participation scheme. There were

various inquiries into the state of British Leyland and the last one—
the Ryder report—recommended workers be involved in
committees along with management to discuss problems outside
the normal sphere.[19] They divided British Leyland into various
negotiating units covering the different plants. A central negotiating
committee covered the whole of British Leyland, usually involving
the convenors from the various plants. Then there were plant committees, made up of works committees and leading stewards from
the various unions in each plant, and area committees, where major
plants like Longbridge were broken into several sections and shop
stewards from each organised into a committee. In Longbridge we
had seven of these local area committees, each of seven workers.
That meant there were 49 people on the committees who became
full-time reps—and that didn't include the works committee members, who, by that time, were also completely full-time.

Where I worked, the committee was supplied with an office
and access to duplicators for producing leaflets and that sort of
thing. But what it meant was that seven shop stewards were taken
away from the people they represented and operated almost as
full-timers inside the plant. I had a period of this myself. You
could go in dressed up and not even bother to take off your coat,
which was ridiculous. It destroyed any connection between the
shop steward and the people on his section. If somebody had a
problem or the section had a problem and the shop steward was
there, involved in it right from the start, it was easy to talk about
it, decide what to do and take it from there. But when there is a
problem and the shop steward is a full-timer sitting on a committee that won't finish meeting until after knocking off time, no one
in a section can even see their steward. When that happens during
an upsurge in militancy, workers can just write off these shop
stewards, go their own way and elect new shop stewards. Or they
can give up and treat the shop stewards as being an arm of management. That was what was beginning to happen in Longbridge
and in the end I had to give up. I finished with the area negotiating
committee and still operated as senior steward. I was on the works
committee, but went only when I was called away for a meeting.
Subsequently I decided with comrades to give that up as well. So I

resigned from the works committee and resigned as leading steward and went back to working on the track.

Breaking of the Longbridge unions: the victimisation of Derek Robinson

At end of 1979 Longbridge convenor Derek Robinson got the sack. Earlier in the year the Leyland Combine Committee (an organisation of shop stewards across Leyland set up by stewards and local officials) had published a pamphlet on the future of Leyland. It was the most anodyne thing.[20] Several months later in November 1979 the management chose to sack Robinson for this pamphlet. It was obvious that they had used him. He was mainly responsible for hammering home the participation scheme with the stewards. Once he had served his purpose, they shat on him. He had done what they wanted, and they wanted rid of him. Sacking Robinson was a symbolic breaking of the union. If they got away with sacking him, management believed they would be able to smash the union organisation in Longbridge. I remember the afternoon it happened we were holding a meeting and somebody came up and said they had sacked Robinson. Nobody believed it until they checked and found it was right. We walked out automatically. But the works committee was calling for a certain amount of restraint. They hoped it was a management bluff or a mistake and they would get him back. It soon became obvious the management weren't bluffing. We called for a strike. It had pretty near solid support in Longbridge. Probably the weakest support was in Robinson's own section. He was a toolmaker and the toolmakers scabbed on the strike to save him. As they saw it, he had sold them down the river when they went on strike.

That toolmakers' strike had taken place across various Leyland plants, including Cowley. The toolmakers struck for restoration of the Coventry agreement that gave toolrooms 10 percent above the average district piece-rate earnings. This had been lost with the introduction of the measured day work scheme and the toolmakers wanted to drop out of the whole measured day work agreement. It was sectional and quite reactionary, but if they had won, it would have destroyed the measured day work scheme and chucked everything into the melting pot again.

Robinson didn't actually cross a picket line. But while they were on strike, he spent much of his time advising the toolroom workers not to strike, to go in and work. He appeared on television, he appeared on the radio, and he gave interviews to every paper from the *Times* to the *Morning Star* attacking his own section.[21] So when Robinson later got the sack, it was his own section who said, "Serves the bastard right." The toolroom workers carried on working. I'm not saying it was a decisive influence in the defeat of the strike, but it played a big part.

Another key factor was that the works committees had lost the will to struggle, particularly at Longbridge. Even when Derek Robinson was sacked and we were on strike, they were trying to calm things down. When I and a couple of SWP[22] members suggested we picket other Leyland plants to bring them out they said, "No, no! Don't do that." We ignored it. The works committee at Longbridge had lost the idea of fighting, lost the ability to fight never mind the desire to fight. So it was left to a carload of SWP members to go to various other plants, including to Cowley in Oxford, to call for support for the strike. Wherever we went we got a sympathetic hearing, but what made it difficult for us was that we were individual stewards without the authority of the works committee, which was deliberately trying to play things cool and not cause trouble.

In the end, one of the biggest factors in ensuring management's success in getting rid of Robinson was the behaviour of the president of his own union.[23] At the end of the strike a march was organised through the centre of Birmingham calling for Robinson's reinstatement. We had local officials from various unions walking on the march with the rest of us—all very impressive. While we were doing this, full-time national members of the various unions were in the plant doing a deal with management. The deal was that he remained sacked. There was the rigmarole of an inquiry, but in reality once people had gone back to work with the guy outside that was the end of it. So Robinson finished up sacked and has been much abused ever since as "Red Robbo" for always leading his members out on strike. In fact he had led a blameless existence, never really supporting militant action, always advocating negotiation rather than strikes.

The decision to pull out of the committees was proved right. The thing I couldn't avoid was that in the process of being proved right I also got older. It became a question of rebuilding from the base but by that time I was retiring and getting my pension.

The downturn in the 1980s: repressing the memory of our power

The general reaction at Longbridge to Thatcher's election in May 1979 was that she would be there for a time and then she would be kicked out. The same thing would happen to her as happened to Ted Heath. People failed to recognise the sapping of the strength of the trade union movement through the move away from struggle to negotiation.

The 1980s were awful compared to the 1970s. All the talk about the awful days of the 1970s is grossly exaggerated. Where there were major struggles in the 1970s, apart from the period 1971-74, they were in the main against management initiatives. So when people talk about the 70s they should be attacking the management, not the trade unions. But there was no doubt militancy dropped off so much in the 1980s that, apart from keeping trade union membership intact, almost everything went by the board.

I believe there was a deliberate policy of getting rid of the older workers who had been through the successful part of the early 1970s. There were offers of reasonable redundancy terms and so on. So many of that generation just couldn't stomach what it was like in the 1980s. They knew how it had been before, so they tended to be glad to accept the redundancies on offer. Management were declaring redundancies at the same time as they were recruiting labour and it was not as though it was for different jobs, for different skills. They were recruiting workers with the same skills as those they were offering redundancy. The government, of course, was a partner of the employers in pushing this through.

Passing on the tools

So in the 1980s, while management were continually eating away at wages and conditions, they were also getting rid of the older layer of those they saw as militants—replacing them with young people: 18, 19, 20. They even tried to introduce kids of 17 onto the track when I was shop steward. After I'd resigned from the works committee I took on the job as shop steward on the first track that they pushed me on. They wanted the 17 year old kids to work on the track night and day when it was supposedly illegal to work nights. That was one of my last flings. I put a stop to it, even though the 17 year olds tried to stop me. They wanted the money. The wages of a 17 year old at Longbridge were that much better than for stacking shelves. In the end, I worked out a situation where the 17 year olds stayed on the track on days learning the different operations and when they were 18 they could take a full job and get the full rate. That struck them as quite good, particularly when at 17 they were on a wage of £70 and when they became 18 they jumped up to £152. It was pretty substantial. But that tended to soften them up as far as management was concerned. When their wages doubled it took some doing to convince them to go on strike.

We got plenty of support when it came to organising solidarity with the miners' strike of 1984-5. It was easy to get money for the miners and the union made a great display of collecting toys for the kiddies in the Christmas of 1984. The miners' wives were invited to speak to the shop stewards' committee. We had probably 400 stewards to listen to Anne Scargill and others of the women. I was more impressed with the women than I was with the Longbridge works committee, although I wasn't particularly impressed with Scargill herself. But the women took it for granted that what they got they had to fight for. That was an attitude that was a bit foreign to the works committee by then.

In my last few years at Longbridge the management buggered me about to get their own back, but I could always sneer and snarl at them because there wasn't a gaffer there who could do a job better than me. I was always defended because I knew how to do a job and they couldn't catch me on that and my timekeeping was fairly good. I wouldn't fall for a sucker punch like being late regularly and that sort of thing. I hadn't got long to go and it got to the stage over the last couple of years where if they had have sacked me they would have had to pay me just as much as if I'd worked up to retirement. So while they were buggering me about, I could still go my own way, do things in my own time and sneer at them. In fact, I developed a quite useful sneer. But if I found the situation bogging me down, picture the effect on people who weren't in a revolutionary party. I could discuss it with other members of our party and take their advice and get out in time. The majority of stewards did not have that, and bear in mind they were all good stewards. When workers elected a steward onto a committee, they did so at a mass meeting. They did not elect numbskulls. They elected the best stewards onto those committees, but the committees were doing what the participation scheme was intended to do. The negotiating committees took the best stewards away from the membership and isolated them until, in the end, not only was the confidence of the shopfloor in the shop steward destroyed, but also the confidence of the shop steward in the shopfloor. The shop stewards began to see their roles as functionaries rather than as representatives of the men.

Postscript to the myth of Red Robbo

Derek Robinson's attitude to me varied according to circumstances. He was a hardline CPer and his attitude towards me could change. A week or two before his sacking I'd been to a meeting along with him and he looked across to me and said if he had an ice pick he'd cheerfully stick it in my skull. But just after he got the sack he found that myself, the SWP and those in the shop stewards meeting who had been most critical of him were the people most active in fighting to keep his job.

The last time I met Derek Robinson was a couple of years back at a meeting. He introduced me as one of his best friends at Longbridge. Memory can be distorted with the passage of time. During the meeting I said that Derek Robinson had in my experience only led one strike in his life. When he spoke afterwards he disagreed with me. He could recall two strikes he had led. But I think one of the strikes he was talking about leading was the strike against his dismissal, which I wouldn't count. The fact was that Robinson and Co had blunted the edge of militancy, so that when the management had sufficient confidence to take on the union structure, Robinson was powerless to stop them. In effect, the shopfloor lost its strength mainly because it had lost confidence in Robinson and the negotiating structures. After Robinson the rank and file and the shopfloor workers managed to keep most of the organisation intact, even though at a much lower level and at a lower level of militancy. But they did manage to keep 100 percent trade unionism. It was the last thing on earth the management thought we'd be able to do. So the rank and file managed to pull one of the chestnuts out of the fire even then.

Conclusion

I became a socialist when the world was engulfed in war. Now it is beset by what appears a series of minor wars. Yet the issues are basically the same and come down to the struggle for domination between rival imperialisms. There has been some change in the contending parties. In 1940 Britain still ranked as a world power. Now it is a junior league player treated with a degree of contempt by US imperialism, which is itself beginning to feel threatened by China.

In many respects, it was easier for imperialism in the 1940s. The US, Britain and Russia could take advantage of the hatred of the Nazis among ordinary working people. It was relatively easy to portray the Second World War as a struggle against fascism and an Allied victory as signifying its destruction. Of course, that was not the case—as anyone connected with Unite Against Fascism or other anti-fascist organisations today can testify. But imperialism has had to find a new enemy. So the wars for oil in Iraq and Afghanistan, the murderous treatment of the Palestinians, the threats against Iran and Syria, are pursued by the world's greatest terrorist—the US—as part of a "war against terror". It is easy to understand how US imperialism, feeling under threat around the world from China, Russia, Japan and Europe and at home from the contradictions within, should respond in a bellicose manner. But why should Britain do the same?

Labourism, in one form or another, has always fulfilled the role of pulling the chestnuts out of the fire for British capitalism—just as trade union leaders have seen their role as negotiating deals that keep the profits of the boss class intact. The Labour Party has sought to protect the wider interests of British capitalism and transfer the costs of this onto the working class. In 1945 it was comparatively easy for the Attlee government to get away with this. The bosses were prepared to tolerate a level of nationalisation that would guarantee supplies of materials and services, and the Labour government could pay compensation far in excess of what the bosses could hope to make in profits under their own management. The capitalists could even accept a National Health Service that would treat people according to need—although this was too much for Tory MPs, who voted against it on every possible occasion.

Most politically conscious workers, like my old man, argued Labour should be given a chance in 1945. It was the first time the party had won an overall majority, and Ramsay MacDonald—who had betrayed Labour and its working class supporters in 1931 by forming a government with the Tories—was dead and gone.

Attlee and Co delivered some reforms, which is more than can be said for the administrations of Blair and Brown. They quickly repealed the Trades Disputes Act, for example, the anti trade union legislation passed by the Tories following the General Strike of 1926. Thatcher's anti trade union legislation remains intact after more than ten years of Labour government—and there lies a difference. Previous Labour leaders have gone out of their way to maintain some links with the trade union movement. Blair went out of his way to destroy those links. It was one of his few successes. The divorce is now so great that it seems to me there is more prospect of bringing socialist ideas and workers together in a different kind of party than in a repeat of the old Labour Party with all its mistakes.

Building new working class organisations will not come easy. Nothing comes easy for the working class. But compared with when I became a socialist the prospects have improved. Instead of a handful of people in a few countries we have at least a handful of people in most cities.

Communication between socialists internationally, which was almost impossible in 1941, is now childishly simple, and the working class has become internationalised to a degree that seemed impossible when I was a youth. No one then would have envisaged China becoming a threat to US capitalism.

The 20th century saw capitalism mad with bloodlust, but also showed it could be stopped in its tracks. In Vietnam, US imperialism was defeated not just by the struggle of the Vietnamese people but by opposition around the world—including in the US. The world's greatest imperial power may now be trying to rid itself of "the Vietnam syndrome", but I look back at the US defeat in Vietnam and other working class victories during my life and view the future with renewed confidence.

I have seen a lot of shifts and changes in the socialist and trade union movement, but nothing that persuades me of a need to change my basic ideas. Globalisation has spread only misery and death across the world. The fact that capitalism appears to be heading into a slump strengthens my feeling that I was right to fight for a socialist future and that there is only one future for the world. I am proud to have played a full part in the struggle for socialism, without which there will be no future for the majority of the world's people. I just wish I was a young 'un.

Above: An article by Frank in *Socialist Worker* in the aftermath of
the Birmingham pub bombings, 1974.
Below: Selling *Socialist Worker* on a picket line.

Afterword

By Matt Perry

Frank's memories are not a historical curiosity or a self-indulgent retrospective for his generation. His activism has relevance today for a world scarred by war and threatened by capitalism's insatiable lust for profit.

One of the problems with biographies is that too often they fail to understand that the forces that shape the lives of their subjects are beyond the reach of any given individual. If in modern times money makes the world go round, Marxists would make the further qualification that the process of amassing investible wealth, or capitalist accumulation, makes our world what it is today. To understand the life of Frank Henderson requires a sense of this. Survival in early human history meant foraging and hunting in communal groups, but survival in the 20th century for employers meant competing for markets, raw materials and profits, and for industrial workers survival meant finding and keeping a job. The cost of failure for the capitalist was bankruptcy and loss of status, for the worker hardship, unemployment and degradation.

This process of capitalist accumulation left its bloodied fingerprints on the last century. Without such an appreciation, Frank's life is reduced to a series of events whose only pattern is that they happened sequentially. Capitalism underwent profound transformations during Frank's lifetime. His father worked in a medium size family-owned factory. The difference between Orme Evans & Co where Frank's dad worked, and the Austin at Longbridge could not be starker. In the 19th century a class of manufacturers owned factories and workshops, and their economic interests were served collectively by parliament and the two main parties, the Liberals and the Conservatives. They channelled their wealth throughout the world via the City of London and the British Empire in the shape of investments, markets and access to raw materials. Through bankruptcies, mergers, acquisitions and the emergence of new industries, riches came to be concentrated in fewer hands. Manufacturers like Herbert Austin and William Morris carried such weight within the economy that they could exert very considerable personal influence upon government.

Not only was wealth being concentrated, but production itself was being revolutionised. The cavernous factories constructed by Austin and Morris—or, for that matter, Citroën and Renault in France, or Ford and Chrysler in the US—stood in stark contrast to the cramped craft-based workshops of Orme Evans. The new factories covered several acres and connected a multiplicity of simple repeated tasks in sequences on assembly lines. All this had subtle and profound effects on the world. It enormously lowered costs, allowing mass production for consumer markets. But the new capacities of large factories also engineered devices for killing on a scale hitherto unimaginable. Not only were larger and more destructive weapons made possible but so too was an increasing and unending supply of arms. And because by the last quarter of the 19th century Britain no longer had global technological and industrial leadership, competitive pressures between firms for profits, markets and sources of investment increasingly became intertwined with military competition between empires. The loss of British manufacturing dominance in the late 19th century overlapped a shift in global patterns of power. After several decades of adjustment and two world wars the British ruling class decided that to maintain a world role it had to play junior partner to US superpower imperialism.

The individual witnessed only small glimpses of these historical trends. The routines and habits of everyday life obscured this overall process, making it seem natural and normal. Change was presented as progress. During Frank's childhood the evidence of this great global transformation was visible in the new housing estates crowding around the aircraft and car plants on the outskirts of Coventry and ceremonies commemorating the dead from the Great War.

In the early part of the 20th century dozens of British car manufacturers competed for a market of well to do consumers in Britain and the empire. But the age of the great manufacturing pioneer was largely eclipsed after the Second World War by the shareholder-owned firm and nationalised industry. The long boom between 1947 and 1973 expanded car ownership from a middle class preserve into the working class. The British car industry was too small a player to compete globally with firms like Ford and General Motors, so the government encouraged a series of mergers that ultimately resulted in British Leyland. Industrial pioneers and owners like Herbert Austin gave way to people like Leyland's boss Michael Edwardes, the epitome of the soulless corporate executive enlisted to rationalise the car industry by closing plants and sacking car workers. In the late 70s and 80s the British car industry underwent a painful restructuring, a product of the declining global profit rates, shifting global patterns of production and investment, together with increasing automation. Despite the hack journalist folklore established in the worst traditions of blaming the victims, the crisis of British car industry was not due to the industrial militancy of the lazy car worker. In the present day era of neoliberalism a dozen or so corporations dominate a now multinational process of production in massively expanded markets for cars that span the globe. In the new millennium UK car manufacturing is conducted by foreign-based firms mainly for British and European markets and has neared the highpoint of output of the early 1970s.[1]

When Frank was a young 'un

The West Midlands—unlike South Wales, Scotland or the north east—was at the heart of the new industries of the 1930s like car, aircraft and tyre manufacturing, with modern methods modelled on those of Henry Ford: the assembly line, the giant workplace and mass production. The older craft metalworking traditions of

Frank's father's generation were giving way to a more modern form of capitalist production.

For Frank, a lad from a family with trade union traditions, his formative years were the period shaped by the General Strike. A long wave of militancy that rose in 1910 crashed in May 1926 when the TUC bureaucracy called off the General Strike, betraying the miners in the process. Union membership collapsed from over six million in 1926 to just over three million in 1933. Thousands were victimised on the railways and in the coalfields. The Trades Disputes Act of 1927 banned solidarity action and general strikes. This was compounded by the slump and mass unemployment of the early 1930s that sapped workers' confidence further and threw many trade unionists onto the dole.

Yet in these barren years future trade union strength germinated. This had little to do with the leaders of the unions who preached cooperation with the employers. Many workers grew impatient with "Mondism", the dirty word for this approach.[2] Earlier memories of rank and file activism revived and workplace organisation was rebuilt from below. The picture varied enormously from one industry to another. In engineering, investment in new giant workplaces in the 1920s and the 1930s posed new challenges for the unions as they often faced fiercely union-busting managements. The unions got a foothold in the giant car plants and tyre factories after historic disputes and tireless work by activists at Pressed Steel, Firestone tyres, Dagenham and Longbridge. In 1937 engineering apprentices' strikes led by young Communists drew younger workers into the unions. Successive apprentices' strikes in engineering and shipbuilding occurred in 1941 and 1944.

The most dynamic force behind this grassroots activity was the Communist Party. From small beginnings its membership, influence and credibility grew considerably during the 1930s. Its members adopted an approach where they would build the confidence of their fellow workers to fight, and when necessary oppose the officials from within the union. Communists had an orientation on the rank and file but not one that was exclusively concerned with the parochial issues of their own workplace. They built the unions in a political way, selling the *Daily Worker* and drawing their colleagues into the mass movements in support of Republican Spain, against the means test and against Oswald Mosley's fascist Blackshirts. They had influence in the rank and file organisation of the shop stewards in the aircraft industry and their newspaper, *The New Propellor*. Frank mentions his brother selling this paper at his workplace. But Frank did not join Communist Party, but the Independent Labour Party and then the Workers' International League, a Trotskyist organisation.

To explain this, we must turn to the politics of the labour movement internationally. In October 1917 the Bolsheviks had come to power as part of a popular revolutionary movement. Their slogans of "Bread, peace and land" and "All power to the soviets [the revolutionary committee movement]" captured the mood of the workers and peasants of Russia. But the new regime was faced with a country devastated by three years of war and industry on the point of collapse. Russia was not a wealthy country and most of its population were impoverished peasants. These were far from ideal circumstances for building a socialist society. Lenin pushed for the revolution in the belief that war-weariness would cause revolution elsewhere in Europe, just as it had in Russia. And it did. But unlike in Russia, revolutions in Germany and Hungary as well as near revolutionary situations elsewhere did not bring about an expanded territory of liberated workers and peasants. The new regime successfully defeated an internal revolt championed by the old Tsarist order and fanned by every imperialist power, but only after more than two years of devastating civil war and famine. It remained isolated internationally. Arguments about the direction of the regime intensified with Lenin's illness and death.

The ultimate victor in these internal upheavals was Stalin, whose policy of "socialism in one country" was opposed by Trotsky. By the late 1920s Stalin's regime had destroyed the last remnants of the workers' revolution of 1917 and was socialist in name only. Its purges, executions, labour camps matched the worst that Western capitalism had to offer, at a time when mass unemployment, fascism and a new arms race led many to yearn for a socialist alternative. From the 1930s two tendencies have dominated the workers' movements across the world, Stalinism and parliamentary reformism. Frank added his youthful voice to the small band of Trotsky's followers who cried out for a world beyond Stalinism and capitalism.

Frank's war

Frank was 14 when the Second World War broke out. The rivalries between empires that had led to the First World War had intensified in the course of the depression, with the defeated powers or those without empires seeking to seize new markets and strategic advantages. In Germany, Hitler, industrialists and aristocratic generals dreamed of turning Russia into their "India" with its abundance of wheat and oil. Mussolini wanted an African empire as well as influence in the Mediterranean to rival the British and French. Fascism in Italy and Germany meant vicious repression of the workers' movements along with a more aggressive foreign policy abroad. Britain and France pursued a policy of appeasement, conceding to German and Italian expansion in central Europe and Ethiopia.

In the Soviet Union, Stalin was concerned with competing militarily with the West and with survival. Any principle could be sacrificed for this end and in late August 1939 a "non-aggression" treaty (known as the Hitler-Stalin pact) between Germany and Russia was signed, secretly allowing these two powers to carve up Poland. The final scene of power-hungry pigs around the table with the farmers in George Orwell's *Animal Farm* drew its inspiration from this pact. Such betrayal of the anti-fascist and anti-imperialist causes sent the Communist Parties of Europe into disarray. They had built their credibility during the 1930s on the basis of anti-fascism, but now Stalin was willing to bargain with Hitler. Russia's socialist prestige was further tarnished when it invaded Finland on 30 November 1939. Stalin's pact with Hitler was not broken until the German invasion of Russia in June 1941.

The first months of war in Britain created an atmosphere of acute social tension and impending catastrophe. Britain, France and its allies suffered one demoralising debacle after another. The German invasion of Norway in April 1940, blundered Allied landings and the German invasion and rapid defeat of France, Belgium and Holland in May and June 1940 brought this sense of crisis to a highpoint. After the defeat at Dunkirk the British government faced a stark choice: to fight on against Hitler or sue for peace. Chamberlain was still in power and was seeking peace. This issue split the Conservative Party and Churchill formed a new coalition government. The Labour Party held major cabinet positions. The war was one of unpredictability, uncertainties and contradictions. Churchill represented that section of the British ruling class that hoped to save the empire by looking across the Atlantic for an ally in the US. For Churchill the war was to defend the empire, but for the Labour left and much of the working class movement it was a war against fascism, a people's war. While many viewed the war in this light and Churchill's government presented it as such with the promise of welfare improvements, others saw it as an imperialist war to re-divide the world just as the Great War had been. This was the case with part of the Independent Labour Party, British Trotskyists and, until the invasion of the Soviet Union in June 1941, the Communist Party.

Looking back at the Second World War in Britain, a powerful mythology obscures popular attitudes of the time. This is most apparent in the hero worship of Churchill who has attracted a veritable industry of biography and celebration. Former Labour minister Mo Mowlam even suggested that Churchill was the greatest Briton of all time: "If Britain—its eccentricity, its big heartedness, its strength of character—has to be summed up in one person, it has to be Winston Churchill." This hazy nostalgic hindsight does not match contemporary views of Churchill, at least among the working class. If Churchill's fierce hostility to strikes had led him to be widely perceived as a committed enemy of British workers, his support for intervention against the early Soviet republic, his use of poison gas and aerial attacks on villages in Afghanistan and Kurdistan, and his parliamentary defence of the Amritsar massacre in India, all earned him reputation as an imperial diehard.[3]

Anecdotal evidence gives glimpses of the complexity of popular attitudes to Churchill. He was booed by many of the 20,000 East

Enders in Walthamstow stadium during the election campaign of 1945, although this was not typical of the general response he received. The Labour Party and many working class people found common ground with Churchill only in his opposition to appeasement and his commitment to war against Nazi Germany. Frank's account brings this out well. Despite the propaganda of common hardships, the war sharpened awareness of social divisions and inequalities of sacrifice and Churchill epitomised cigar-smoking top-hatted inherited privilege.[4] Rationing presented the image of egalitarianism, but the wealthy could circumvent this through either the black market or legally by going to upmarket hotels like the Ritz and Savoy which remained open and where the rich were able to dine on whatever they liked. The working class of London's East End and the industrial areas of Britain bore the brunt of the "Blitz", the Luftwaffe's bombing campaign, while the upper class could escape to country houses. When children were evacuated, they were often treated very badly by their reluctant social superiors who housed them.

While Labour joined Churchill's coalition cabinet and helped promote a wartime consensus that promised great reforms at the war's end, there was considerable disquiet inside the working class over a string of issues, from the lack of air raid shelters, the political truce in by-elections, the release from prison of Oswald Mosley in October 1943 and restrictions on workers' rights. With Labour in the coalition government, and—from June 1941— Communist Party support for the war effort, the trade union bureaucracy fully supported increased production and discouraged strikes. Joint production committees between management and trade union representatives sought to raise output. In these circumstances, as Frank notes, there was a political space for the far left. His organisation, the Trotskyist Workers' International League, from tiny beginnings grew rapidly and related to a number of important workplace struggles such as the Tyneside apprentices' strikes of 1944.

For those coming into political awareness in the late 1930s, it was clear that history was heading towards the catastrophe of world war for a second time. The dazzling technological achievements of modern capitalism would bring the terror of war to every civilian, to every home in Europe. Frank's family were no exception. Although "the Blitz" is popularly associated with the East End of London, the German bombing campaign particularly targeted industrial and working class areas right across the country. Coventry, where Frank was living at the time, was one of its worst victims.

The contradiction between the rhetoric of a people's war and the reality of a war for empire was evident in all the theatres of military operations that Frank was sent to. At the war's end British armed forces were engaged in colonial policing in the attempt to reconstruct the empire, while inside Europe they ensured the restabilisation of capitalism. Indeed, Churchill's coalition and Attlee's post-war Labour government deployed troops to occupy and, if necessary, wage war against local resistance movements aimed at national independence. This repression even entailed doing deals with some of those who had fought for the Axis powers. Although Frank was sent to Italy, Greece and Palestine, he might equally have been sent to Aden, Malaya or Indonesia. The picture would have been similar. In Greece, Italy and France—where Communists had played a significant role in resistance movements—the British and American governments feared that resistance movements would install workers' power in the factories and bring radical change to the countryside. Stalin, for his part, did everything in his power to make sure that this did not occur.

The Allies had landed in Sicily in July 1943 and the invasion created a crisis for Mussolini's regime. King Victor Emmanuel—who had appointed Mussolini as prime minister in 1922 and remained the head of state—replaced the fascist leader with Marshall Badoglio. Despite Badoglio's record as a loyal fascist, the Allies were willing to negotiate peace with him and recognise his government. But beginning with a strike wave in northern Italy in March 1943, a mass resistance movement developed against Italian and German fascism. The Germans occupied northern Italy, installing Mussolini in a puppet regime. Anti-fascist partisans in the North fought a bitter and bloody battle. With the advance of Allied troops, the partisans liberated several Italian cities, and Mussolini was captured and strung up in a square in Milan. After agreement over East-West spheres of European influence with Stalin, the troops of Britain and America remained to ensure that the partisans did not take power and that the new Italian regime stayed in their camp. When Frank arrived in the summer of 1945, the Italian Communist Party was still a member of the coalition government and local partisans' taste of victory against fascism was still sweet. For that brief share of power, the Italian Communist Party abandoned the possibility of socialist revolution. The memory of its role in the resistance, however, meant that for decades it was the largest Communist Party in Western Europe.

In Greece, Frank's next posting, there was a similar clash between a popular anti-fascist resistance and the great power politics of the Allies. A mass guerrilla army, ELAS (People's Liberation Army of Greece), fought the Italian and German occupiers. By 1943 the resistance movement, EAM (National Liberation Front)/ELAS, had liberated four fifths of Greece. The Communist Party was pivotal to the formation of ELAS and its political wing, EAM. As part of the agreement between Churchill and Stalin of October 1944, however, Greece was to be within the British sphere of influence, unlike much of Eastern Europe which was designated to be within the Russian orbit. Given the character of ELAS, Churchill was determined to exclude it from power and promote Britain's Greek allies: the Greek royal family, the royalist EDES (Greek Democratic People's League) and those connected with the dictator Metaxas.

When the Germans left in October 1944, British troops entered Greece. Churchill told General Scobie, "The clear objective is the defeat of EAM." Scobie demanded that ELAS lay down their arms but refused to call for the Greek right wing movement EDES, which had a dubious resistance record, to lay down theirs. This incensed the resistance fighters as the right had collaborated for a time with the Nazis in trying to destroy ELAS. The new government even incorporated many of the pro-Nazi militia—the Security Battalions—into the police. EAM in Athens called a demonstration on 2 December 1944. The police fired on the unarmed demonstration, which included many women and children, killing at least ten, many citing a figure of 28. This started the "December events", a spontaneous battle for Athens. This flared into an armed insurrection which threatened to overthrow the new British-sponsored regime. Only after several weeks and the drafting in of reinforcements were British troops able to suppress ELAS, using aircraft to strafe and artillery to bombard their positions in the suburbs of Athens. On the day after the Yalta conference between Stalin, Roosevelt and Churchill the Varkiza agreement of 12 February signalled the cessation of fighting. The seeds of the second Greek civil war of 1947-9 had been sown. The new provisional Greek regime started to intern ELAS fighters. British troops remained in Greece until February 1947. It was in the context of vicious repression of the left and a Communist Party boycott that the elections of March 1946 and the referendum on the monarchy of November 1946 took place. Throughout this entire process, not wishing to upset the post-war settlement, Stalin offered little or no support to Greek Communists. As John Newsinger observes, "Greece was the only country occupied by the Axis where after the war collaboration went unpunished and resistance was criminalised".[5]

Finally, Frank was sent to Palestine. During the First World War foreign minister Arthur Balfour (who had introduced the anti-semitic Aliens Act of 1905) had stated that Britain would support the establishment of a Jewish homeland in Palestine. Zionist Chaim Weizmann had persuaded the British cabinet that Jewish settlers would act in the interests of the empire, especially through control over the vital Suez Canal, by undermining the challenge of Arab nationalism. Britain fostered Jewish settlement and armed the Zionist militias to supplement its own forces to thwart Palestinian resistance.

The Holocaust of European Jewry, the darkest moment in capitalism's history, once again revealed the contradictions of the Second World War and the ensuing peace. As the Nazis retreated, one death camp after another was liberated by the Allies, releasing large numbers of displaced and homeless Jews desperate for a safe refuge and a new life. With US borders firmly closed to the majority and encouraged by Zionists, many saw Palestine as the only option. With the relative decline of British power and the radicalisation of elements of Zionism, the Zionists militias now turned on

the British and seeking to push them out and establish an independent Zionist state. The militias turned to terrorist attacks on the
British, culminating in the bombing of the King David Hotel on 22
July 1946. Within a year or so of Frank's tour of duty in Palestine
the UN established the state of Israel and these very same militias
capitalised on the situation to seize land from the Palestinians.[6]

Post-war Britain

When Frank returned to Britain, political circumstances had
changed fundamentally. The Labour government, swept to power
by a spectacular landslide in June 1945, was the first Labour
administration to possess a parliamentary majority. There were
high expectations for change from its supporters. Of all the Labour
governments, Attlee's period in office delivered the most significant
reforms. It extended secondary schooling, created the NHS and
nationalised the coal industry, the railways, gas and electricity. For
some inside the Labour movement, this is still seen as the golden
age of the party. Despite this nostalgia, Labour's record is not as
impressive as it might seem. First, for much of the period working
class people had to put up with continued rationing and hardship
as the economy, presided over by former left winger Sir Stafford
"Austerity" Cripps, strained to supply the empire with troops. Second, many of reforms were not born of a radical socialist
programme determined to put wealth and power into the hands of
working people but came directly from the wartime coalition with
the Tories. Clement Attlee's government shelved elements of its programme that stretched the consensus of mainstream politics too far,
leading, for example, to the resignation of Nye Bevan over the
introduction of charges in the NHS. Third, the Labour government
was not just willing to use troops to repress movements for
national independence in the colonies but also to break strikes at
home. Finally, it secretly developed a British atomic bomb. When
the Conservatives returned to office in 1951, where they remained
for the next 13 years, they did not reverse Labour's reforms.
Instead a pro-welfare consensus marked official politics in condi-

tions where industrialised capitalist countries enjoyed 20 years of unprecedented growth, full employment, increasing living standards and generous (by historical standards) welfare provision.

The Labour Party was, at this time, a vibrant mass party that was able to deliver local reforms, in particular council housing. Unlike today, it was an organisation with vital roots in the associational culture of the working class and there was real political life inside its structures. With these deep roots and the possibility of reforms, there was no space for a left electoral alternative to Labour or any notion of unions disaffiliating from the party.

Capitalism's long post-war boom also created the conditions where trade union organisation could patiently build its power by securing concessions that employers could afford. Areas previously hostile to unions now became transformed into bastions of trade unionism. This was true above all in the car industry. Before the Second World War, Longbridge, later a byword for union militancy, had been 90 percent non-union. After 1940 trade union activists had little fear of losing their jobs because unemployment was so low. The shop steward was the key to these improvements and the trade union bureaucracy of full-time officials could not ignore the membership. Quite often, as Frank observes, the very opposite was the case. By 1979 there were 350,000 shop stewards in Britain.

Earthquakes in the East

1956 was a key year for the remaking of the revolutionary left internationally. On 25 February the Soviet leader Nikita Khrushchev delivered his "secret speech" to the 20th Congress of the Communist Party of the Soviet Union. In it he denounced Stalin's crimes, the gulags—labour camps—and the cult of personality. Arguments at the top of the Stalinist states created a space for protest from below. Riots in Poznan, Poland, were followed much more dramatically by a workers' revolution against Stalinism in Hungary. This was eventually crushed by Soviet tanks with 20,000 Hungarians killed. The repression generated

shockwaves within the Communist Parties outside the Eastern
bloc. The *Daily Worker*'s Budapest correspondent Peter Fryer
described the events as an authentic workers' revolution and
broke with the CP. The British party suffered an epidemic of res-
ignations, losing nearly a third of its members.[7] For the emerging
New Left these events reignited debates about both the possibility
of revolution centred on the working class and the bankruptcy of
Stalinism as a force for such change. One strand of this emerging
left was the small Socialist Review Group around Tony Cliff
(later they became known as the International Socialists) who
subscribed to the analysis of the Soviet Union as a state capitalist
power, where the state acted as a single capitalist employer locked
into competitive (especially military) accumulation with its Western rivals.[8] Cliff's group was opposed to both imperialisms, East
and West, at a time when the overwhelming majority of the left
lined up, whatever their reservations, behind one or other side in
the Cold War.

The 1970s: workers' revolt and the end of the post-war consensus

Labour was returned to government in 1964. The party soon dis-
appointed the hopes for radical change that had accompanied its
victory. Within a couple of years it was attempting to defeat a seafarers' dispute and to impose an incomes policy. Even worse from
a trade union standpoint, Barbara Castle's white paper *In Place of
Strife* proposed legislation that would undermine the power of
rank and file trade union organisation by secret ballots, fines and
cooling off periods. Although anticipating the anti-union legislation under the Tories, Barbara Castle presented the white paper as
a left wing move, as she perversely characterised unofficial action
as breaking the principles of working class solidarity. This set the
scene for the wave of industrial militancy that swept Britain from
1968 to 1974.

   Journalistic cliché now turned historical wisdom tells us that the
unions had grown too powerful in the 1970s. The industrial conflict of the 1970s was more complex. It was rooted in economic

crisis and the desire of the successive governments and the employers to shift the balance of power in industry dramatically in their favour. From the late 1960s right through to the Thatcher governments there were periodic efforts to shackle the ability of shop stewards and the rank and file of trade unions from securing their own interests. Disguised in the press as the defence of British liberties or the only hope for British industry, this concerted attack on the unions shaped Frank's later working life and so many others like him.

British capitalism had for several decades undergone a relative decline compared to its major rivals such as Japan and West Germany, whose investment rates were higher and consequently also their productivity. Already during the 1960s wage freezes had hit working class families and job losses threatened various industries such as the National Coal Board's programme of pit closures. The book produced by the International Socialists that Frank mentions—Tony Cliff's *The Employers' Offensive*—explained the connections between productivity deals, the difficulties of British capitalism and the employers' offensive against the unions. The global economic slowdown of the late 1960s and the two world recessions of the 1970s increased the pressure on governments to undertake such measures. The prognosis of the financial experts was that a brutal process of restructuring was required. Despite their forecasts, to the contrary it was obvious that the price for this would be paid by workers in manufacturing and mining industries. This restructuring would throw millions of workers out of a job, turn parts of the country into industrial wastelands and destroy the fabric of many working class communities. The principal obstacle to this happening was the tradition of rank and file organisation and industrial militancy of British workers. By 1968 there were 175,000 shop stewards in engineering alone.

The 1970s opened with a shock election defeat for Wilson. Like him, Ted Heath, the Conservative prime minister, sought to reverse the decline of British capitalism by making workers pay. Efforts to break the power of the unions dominated his government. His Industrial Relations Bill drew on and extended the recommendations of *In Place of Strife*. The Conservative government also presided over rising unemployment, cut tax for the rich and squeezed public spending. This combination of an employer and government offensive against working class living standards increasingly met a militant response. From the start the Industrial Relations Bill brought protest, and although the TUC sought to avoid strike action, the Communist Party led body, the Liaison Committee for the Defence of Trade Unions, did succeed in pulling off some walkouts.

Industrial militancy found expression in the six-week miners' strike of January-February 1972, which was the first national strike in the coal industry since 1926 and used the tactics of mass and fly- ing pickets outside coking plants, power stations and steelworks. The crucial moment in the dispute was the closure of the Saltley depot in Birmingham, which Frank recalls vividly in his account. It was an embarrassing defeat for the government. That year also wit- nessed a wave of occupations in engineering factories centred on Manchester and Sheffield. The militancy spilled out from the work- place into rent strikes, school student strikes and prisoners taking protest action.

The government counted upon their new legislation to bring the workers to heel. The test of Heath's Industrial Relations Act came with the jailing of five dockers in the summer of 1972. The "Pentonville Five", as they became known, were jailed for picket- ing a storage depot of containers that were not unloaded by registered dockers. The picket line had a profound role in trade union struggles and was a symbol of the collective power and sol- idarity of working people. With the mood of self-confidence and the sense of tradition under attack, the imprisonment sent a surge of adrenalin through the ranks of trade union activists. With the reluctance of the trade union leaders to act, the Liaison Committee for the Defence of Trade Unions provided a network through which a strike wave generalised. By the time the government extracted itself from the situation by freeing the Pentonville Five, there was in effect an unofficial general strike sweeping the coun- try. The Industrial Relations Act was dead.[9] When the miners launched a second national strike in 1974, Heath sought refuge in a general election, calculating that an endorsement of his government would fatally undermine the strike. His election slogan "Who governs Britain?" met the response, "Not bloody you!"

In the wave of militancy during the Heath years the International Socialists (IS) transformed themselves from a largely student organisation of under 1,000 members to an organisation four times the size with a strong working class element. It initiated a national rank and file movement and established factory branches where it had sufficient members, such as at Longbridge. The Communist Party had been the principal organisation that had attempted to build in the shop stewards movement. Having formally abandoned revolution in Harry Pollitt's *The British Road to Socialism* (1951), it sought to encourage wage militancy and get Communists elected to official positions within the trade union movement, and it did so with some success, especially in the electricians' union (ETU), until it was ousted in a vote-rigging scandal in 1961. In the mid-1960s it changed its strategy from attempting to get Communists elected to efforts to build broad lefts with Labour lefts to get left wingers elected (such as Jack Jones at the TGWU, Hugh Scanlon of the AEU and Lawrence Daly of the NUM). Despite considerable influence in workplaces like Longbridge, the CP was a shrinking organisation and continued to decline because of its Stalinist politics during the workers' revolt in the early 1970s.[10] IS, on the other hand, formed dozens of factory branches, established rank and file newspapers like the *Carworker*, *The Collier* and *The Hospital Worker*, and in March 1974 launched a national Rank and File Movement.[11]

The Labour government of 1974 came to power on a mood of militancy and deployed radical rhetoric to capture this widespread sentiment. It introduced progressive legislation such as the Equal Pay Act, which claimed to end pay discrimination against women, although it took a rash of strikes to enforce the Act's provisions. However, Labour's term in office coincided with the sharpest recession since the 1930s and, according to the logic of reformism, Labour looked to manage capitalism responsibly. Rather than repeating the debacle of the Industrial Relations Act, it sought the cooperation of the trade union bureaucracy in what it termed the social contract, or what others more perceptively dubbed the "social con-trick". This entailed left trade union leaders such as the "terrible twins" of Hugh Scanlon and Jack Jones holding their memberships back and arguing for wage restraint in conditions of rising lay-offs and inflation. Trade union leaders condemned strike action and even argued with their members to cross picket lines. The essential truth learned through bitter experience, that without solidarity the working class is powerless, was ignored by trade union leaders who were more concerned with appeasing Labour prime ministers Harold Wilson and James Callaghan.

Labour's efforts at wage restraint and the real cuts in working class living standards that resulted finally collapsed in 1978 with the so-called "Winter of Discontent". Just as lazy car workers were blamed for the ills of the British motor industry, so the low paid were blamed for the defeat of the Labour government in the general election of 1979. This ubiquitous myth served the interests of both Labour and Conservative politicians. The unions were too powerful and it was the left that was responsible for the problems of the country. It has been the standard line recycled by Thatcherites, Labour "modernisers" and journalists ever since. Instead what happened was that working class living standards were sharply eroded and unemployment shattered the lives of millions. Union leaders were able to prevent opposition to the social contract until 1978 when the mounting pressure eventually found its release. The low paid could wait no more and struck. They were condemned by "their" government—one that had betrayed them. The balance sheet of the Labour government makes grim reading. Coming to power on the back of high hopes, rank and file exuberance and promises of radical reform, it exited having cut the NHS at the bidding of the International Monetary Fund, made scabbing respectable and profoundly demoralised the ranks of the labour movement. Under Labour, British fascism in the shape of the National Front once again threatened to become a mass movement. Thatcher's orchestrated plans to attack the unions one by one are now well known, but the secret of her success against the organised working class in the 1980s is that her path had been scouted by the Labour government of 1974-79.

Thatcher and the workers' retreat to the present

When Margaret Thatcher was elected in 1979, it was not the turning point that many retrospectively believed it to be. It was Callaghan who was the first chancellor of the exchequer to abandon the Keynesian idea of full employment and try to hold down the money supply. The first post-war attempts to "rationalise" British manufacturing through massive lay-offs came under Labour. Even the anti-union stance was clearly visible in the Labour government's attitude to the low paid who had the temerity to try to prevent their real wages from falling. The "unions are too powerful", the rallying cry of Thatcher, confused two distinct phenomena. The first—the traditions of rank and file militancy and strike action—peaked in the early 1970s. The second was the high level relationship between government and union leaders, infamously visiting Downing Street for beer and sandwiches, and the influence of trade union leaders on the Labour Party via the trade union block vote at Labour Party conference. That second dimension of union power was used between 1974 and 1979 to *restrain* attempts by workers to maintain real wages and fight redundancies. The story inside Longbridge bears this out.

The demise of trade union militancy at Longbridge resulted from a number of elements. First, management had a strategy of marginalising shop stewards in the process of wage determination and of incorporating them in bargaining structures that would separate them from the shopfloor. Frank explains that measured day work and the participation schemes were the employers' means to do this. Second, union officials helped to tame industrial militancy. In Longbridge it was the role of the Communist Party and the plant's convenor of the shop steward's committee, Derek Robinson, that was critical. Management could not have succeeded without Red Robbo's endorsement of participation. In so doing, as Frank shows Robinson thereby unwittingly prepared his own undoing. When Longbridge management concocted a case for his sacking, the unions at Longbridge proved incapable of reversing his victimisation. Only a couple of years before, this would have been unthinkable. Rank and file activity and solidarity which had been the secret of the workers' revolt of the early 70s had been undermined from within.

But these strategies could only prove successful because of wider weaknesses inside the working class movement. The loyalty of the union leaders, left and right, to the Labour government (and the unwillingness of the Communist Party to seriously challenge this) opened the door to arguments about the need to protect the "viability" and "profitability" of business by holding back workers' demands. In the boom years after the war the reformist ideas held by most militants (and as Frank shows, sometimes even more right wing ideas) in no way acted to curtail workers' militancy in key parts of industry. The situation by the late 70s had altered considerably. Now politics was crucial in shaping workers' response to the crisis. The radicalisation of the late 60s and early 70s had opened a space for revolutionary ideas inside the British working class in way not seen since the 1920s. But it not been enough to create a mass revolutionary force capable of decisively challeging the Communist Party and beyond that the influence of Labourism. This now proved the achilles heel of the British working class.

The 1980s was a period when the balance of power shifted quite appreciably to the employers. The Thatcher government embarked on an ambitious project of destroying union power. Taking on unions and industries one at a time—according to a strategy mapped out in the "Ridley plan"—her government defeated in turn steel workers, miners, print workers, seafarers and dockers. These defeats were not inevitable and each fight showed the potential to reverse the retreat. Unemployment grew to devastating levels, exacerbated by very high interest rates and monetarist dogma. Mass joblessness undermined workers' confidence and corroded communities. These were years of downturn for workers, which was reinforced by the failure of the TUC to deliver solidarity action, and the shift to the right of Labour under Neil Kinnock. The years of Thatcherism exacted a heavy price on the British working class. Manufacturing industry contracted considerably. In such circumstances the horizons of workplace activists changed. In Longbridge the key task was maintaining union membership and teaching younger workers trade union traditions. When Frank retired in

1990, despite ten years of management pressure Longbridge remained a union shop.

Historically, the British working class has been through several periods of recomposition—when older industries decline and newer ones take their place—and defeat. The composition of generations, gender, geography and ethnicity undergoes profound changes, as do the points of political reference. These periods, like the 1860s and 1870s, or the 1930s, or the 1980s and 1990s, have been followed by recovery and the emergence of new patterns of trade union militancy and working class politics. On each occasion the traditions of previous generations informed that rebirth. It is the potential contribution of Frank and his generation of activists to the renewal of workers' struggle and socialist politics that makes this book significant. More than that, his experiences of workers' militancy in his native West Midlands, in Italy, in Greece and in Algeria point to the revolutionary potential of ordinary people to wrestle capitalism to the ground and free humanity from its stifling embrace once and for all. As his memoirs testify, Frank is a working class thinker, not only an activist but also someone whose Marxist understanding of the world has allowed him to participate in its transformation and lay the groundwork for the next generation to take up the fight.

Notes

One: Youth

1 Frank was born 13 February 1925.

2 Shadow factories were set up as part of the rearmament drive as a partnership between the government and private industry.

3 In 1935 the Communist Party launched a rank and file organisation for the aircraft industry, the Aircraft Shop Stewards National Council. *New Propellor* was its newspaper.

4 At this point in the interview Frank recited the poem from memory at double speed.

5 In January 1936 George V died and was succeeded by his son Edward VIII. Before his coronation, however, he sparked a constitutional crisis over his love affair with an American divorcee, Wallis Simpson. There are also suspicions that the couple's fascist sympathies may have played some role in the conflict. After a certain amount of brinkmanship, Edward abdicated in December but this created a public furore as the crisis had been kept from the papers until that moment. His younger brother George VI then came to the throne.

6 The Munich Agreement between Britain, France, Germany and Italy was signed on 29 September 1938. It was the high point of the Franco-British policy of appeasement of the fascist powers and Hitler was handed a significant part of democratic Czechoslovakia. Appeasement led to those politicians who were identified with to be discredited.

Two: War and the revolutionary

1 Three British cruisers engaged the *Graf Spee*, the German pocket battleship, at the Battle of the River Plate on 13 December 1939. Damaged and cornered in Montevideo, the captain scuttled his own ship four days later.

2 Germany invaded Norway on 9 April 1940. In response, the British-French landing was a fiasco. Churchill was the First Lord of the Admiralty at the time.

3 During Germany's defeat of France in late May 1940 the British Expeditionary Force fighting alongside the French retreated and the decision was taken to withdraw the army from the continent. Stranded on the Dunkirk coastline, a flotilla of private vessels assisted in the official evacuation of British troops. Great propaganda about

the "Dunkirk spirit" was made of
this. News of the evacuation was
not published in the press until
three days after its beginning. It
was a military defeat dressed up as
a victory of "British pluck".

4   The two British politicians most
tainted by appeasement of Hitler
were Neville Chamberlain, the
Conservative prime minister
(November 1937 to May 1940),
and Lord Halifax, his foreign
secretary (February 1938 to
December 1940).

5   Conservative Anthony Eden had
resigned as foreign secretary in
February 1938 over the question of
appeasement. He was reappointed
to the same post in December
1940, replacing Lord Halifax.

6   Winston Churchill was the home
secretary during a miners' strike in
South Wales during 1910-11. The
police killed a miner in Tonypandy
during disturbances and Churchill
then sent troops to quell the
unrest. His brutal repression was
deeply implanted into the folk
memory of South Wales and
British workers more generally.

7   Eccentric farmer Hancock polled
10,488 votes. Churchill's majority
was 17,200.

8   Herbert Morrison was the home
secretary during Churchill's
wartime coalition government and
a leading member during Attlee's
Labour government of 1945-51.
Controversially, after having
banned the *Daily Worker* despite
its wartime patriotism, he sought
to close down the *Daily Mirror* in
1942-3 but failed when this led to
a debate in the House of
Commons. He was also the subject
of campaigning when he decided

to release the fascist Oswald
Mosley from prison in 1943.

9   William Beveridge's report was
published in 1942 (its official name
was the Social Insurance and Allied
Services report). It had been
commissioned by Churchill's
coalition government to investigate
social policy and sought to fight the
five "giant evils" of "want, disease,
ignorance, squalor and idleness". It
was a key to persuading British
people that real social change
would follow the war.

10 Penguin and Pelicans were a series
of publications aimed at
popularising contemporary issues
in politics, sciences and the arts.

11 The Clarion cycling club was
formed by socialists in 1895. Lord
Haw Haw, William Joyce, had
been deputy leader of Oswald
Mosley's British Union of Fascists.
He went to Germany and
broadcast propaganda for the
Third Reich during the Second
World War. He was hanged as a
traitor in 1946.

12 H G Wells was a Fabian socialist—
a moderate brand of socialist
thought influential in the Labour
Party which equated socialism with
state ownership—a playwright and
science fiction writer.

13 The ILP was formed in 1893 after
the election of Keir Hardie to
Westminster from West Ham as
the first independent labour
representative. It was part of the
Labour Party until 1932. It had
four MPs after the 1935 election.

14 In 1939 the Foreign Office charged
the British Consulate in Los
Angeles with investigating
Chaplin's film and the consul
interviewed him to express the

government's opposition to the film. The Foreign Office also contacted the British Board of Film Censors and there were plans to censor the film. By the time of its release the government's policy of appeasement was over and Britain was at war with Germany. For more see K R M Short, "Documents: Chaplin's 'The Great Dictator' and British censorship, 1939", *Historical Journal of Film, Radio and Television*, vol 5, no 1, 1985, pp85-108.

15 Chaplin was writing the script in 1939 but changed the script to include the final speech after the invasion of France. United Artists wrote to him stating it would not be shown in Britain or the US.

16 Chaplin's speech included: "...Then in the name of democracy let's use that power—let us all unite. Let us fight for a new world, a decent world that will give men a chance to work, that will give you the future and old age and security. By the promise of these things, brutes have risen to power, but they lie. They do not fulfill their promise. They never will. Dictators free themselves but they enslave the people. Now let us fight to fulfill that promise. Let us fight to free the world, to do away with national barriers, do away with greed, with hate and intolerance. Let us fight for a world of reason, a world where science and progress will lead to all men's happiness."

17 A Trotskyist paper, the forerunner of the Workers' International League's *Socialist Appeal*.

18 The Left Book Club (1936-48) was initially a joint venture between the Communist Party and the left wing publisher Victor Gollancz. It commissioned and popularised socialist literature such as George Orwell's *The Road to Wigan Pier* and Ellen Wilkinson's *The Town That Was Murdered*. At its peak it had nearly 60,000 members.

19 Norman Angell was the author of the anti-war treatise *The Great Illusion* (1909) and various other works. He later became a Labour MP. The popular front was the policy of the Communist International established at its seventh congress in 1935 which advocated electoral and anti-fascist alliances between workers' organisations and "progressive" bourgeois forces.

20 The left wing American journalist John Reed's classic eyewitness account of the Russian Revolution of 1917. The 1981 film *Reds*, with Warren Beatty, was based on Reed's life.

21 Between late August 1939 and 22 June 1941, a non-aggression pact, known as the Hitler-Stalin pact, between Nazi Germany and the Soviet Union was in place which allowed each power to seize territories from smaller powers such as Poland and Finland without fear of intervention from the other. Both the signing and the breaking of the pact pushed the Communist Parties into humiliating policy U-turns.

22 This pamphlet can be found at http://www.marxists.org/history/international/comintern/sections/britain/clear-them-out/index.htm

23 The *New Leader* was the paper of the ILP.

24 A fourth edition was printed in 1941 and there is a copy in the

London School of Economics library.

25 Trotsky was attacked in Mexico City by Ramon Mercader, a Stalinist agent on 20 August 1940, dying in hospital the following day. See "Trotsky Murdered", *Workers' International News*, vol 3, no 9, September 1940 and "Leading Mexican Stalinists Implicated in Trotsky's Murder", *Workers' International News*, vol 3, no 11, November 1940.

26 Alexandra Kollontai (1872-1952), Russian revolutionary, was elected to the Bolshevik Central Committee in 1917, becoming Commissar of Public Welfare after the revolution. She was part of the opposition to the rightward transformation of the Soviet regime during the 1920s but later conformed and took up a number of official ambassadorial and diplomatic posts. She is perhaps best known for her writings on Marxism and women's liberation.

27 Ted Grant was later one of the founders of the Militant Tendency.

28 Jock Haston (1913-86), a leading figure in the WIL and later the Revolutionary Communist Party.

29 The Militant Workers' Federation was initiated by the WIL in 1943 as an attempt to group together industrial militants opposed to the policy of class collaboration promoted during the war by the Labour Party leadership, trade union leaders and the Communist Party.

30 Royal Ordnance Factories were government-owned factories that produced war materials until privatisation in 1987.

31 Sam Bornstein and Al Richardson,

War and the International: A History of the Trotskyist Movement in Britain, 1937-1949 (*Socialist Platform*, London, 1986).

32 The unofficial Tyne Apprentices' Guild had organised the strikes of Tyneside apprentices in late March 1944. Bill Davy had been expelled from the Communist Party and was in touch with Roy Tearse, the industrial organiser of the WIL. The apprentices threatened to strike against conscription to mining duties. At its height over 7,000 Tyneside apprentices in shipbuilding and engineering were on strike; apprentices on the Clyde and in Huddersfield also joined the strike. See Richard Croucher, *Engineers at War* (Merlin, London, 1983), pp230-239 and Sam Bornstein and Al Richardson, as above, pp115-147.

33 Those imprisoned were Heaton Lee (12 months), Ann Keen (13 days), Roy Tearse (12 months) and Jock Haston (6 months).

34 The Anti-Labour Laws' Victims' Defence Committee was launched on 9 May in Conway Hall with speakers including MPs Jimmie Maxton, John McGovern and W G Cove.

35 Paul Foot (1937-2004), acclaimed journalist, SWP member and nephew of Michael Foot.

36 The partisans were the mass armed resistance movement that developed during 1943 and 1944.

37 In July 1943 the Italian King Victor Emmanuel III replaced Mussolini with Field Marshall Pietro Badoglio as prime minister. Badoglio surrendered to the Allies on 8 September. But the Germans installed Mussolini as leader of the

north of the country in the "Republic of Salo" and continued to fight the Allied advance and the Italian resistance movement. Badoglio had headed Italian forces during the invasion of Abyssinia (1935-6) and approved of the use of poison gas.

38 Field Marshall (Later Viscount) Sir Bernard Montgomery, "Monty", supposedly popular with the troops, made his reputation at the victory over Rommel's Africa corps at El-Alamein in October-November 1942. He commanded Allied forces involved in the invasion of France between June and August 1944.

39 The Italian Communist Party, in line with Stalin's agreement that Italy would remain under the Western influence after the war, opposed any moves towards socialist revolution and even cooperated with the Allies in handing over arms held by the resistance. See Tom Behan, *The Long Awaited Moment: The Working Class and the Italian Communist Party in Milan, 1943-1948* (Peter Lang, New York, 1997), and Paul Ginsborg, *A History of Contemporary Italy: Society and Politics: 1943-1988* (Penguin, 1990).

40 The Greek Communist Party, which had been central to the resistance to the fascist occupation of Greece, called for an abstention in these elections. In the polarised atmosphere of impending civil war, the right won the general election (31 March 1946) and the monarchy was re-established after a referendum boycotted by the Communists (1 November 1946). See John Newsinger, *British*

Intervention and the Greek Revolution (Socialist History Society, 2002).

41 The Allied Mission to Observe the Greek Elections was formed out of the ceasefire of 12 February 1945 to end the fighting between ELAS and the British and EDES. There were 240 teams of a British, French or American observer (often an army officer), a jeep driver and an interpreter.

42 Ioannes Metaxas was the Greek dictator from 1936 until 1941. Italy invaded Greece in October 1940 but was defeated in April 1941. German, Italian and Bulgarian forces then occupied Greece.

43 Navy, Army and Air Force Institutes (NAAFI) were clubs, canteens and shops for military personnel.

44 Duncan Hallas was a member of the WIL and later of the International Socialists and SWP (1925-2002). He took part in soldiers' strikes in Egypt as they waited for demobilisation. http:// www.socialistworker.co.uk/ art.php?id=4605

45 After the First World War and the break-up of the Ottoman Empire, Palestine was under British rule as a "mandate" from the League of Nations. The British encouraged Jewish settlement which led to increasing antagonism between Zionist settlers and Palestinians. In 1936 when the Palestinians staged a general strike the British used the army and airforce against the strikes and encouraged Zionist militias to attack the Palestinians.

46 Irgun was a Zionist terrorist organisation hostile to British rule.

It was led by Menachem Begin, who later became Israeli prime minister (1977-83). It was responsible for the explosion at the King David Hotel on 22 July 1946 that claimed 92 lives.

47 On 5 July 1945 Clement Attlee's Labour Party was elected to office with a majority of 147 seats. It had formed a government on two occasions before in 1924 and 1929-31, but on both occasions it had to rely on Liberal support because it did not have a parliamentary majority.

Three: Post-war Britain

1   The Revolutionary Communist Party had been formed in March 1944 when the Workers' International League and the Revolutionary Socialist League merged with the encouragement of the International Secretariat of the Fourth International, principally the American Trotskyists.

2   Gerry Healy (1913-89), later the founder of the Socialist Labour League and the Workers' Revolutionary Party.

3   After a split in the RCP in 1947 over whether to enter the Labour Party, Healy's faction secretly worked within the Labour Party.

4   *Socialist Outlook* was published by the Socialist Fellowship between 1948 and 1954 when it was closed down by the Labour Party's National Executive Committee. It was edited by John Lawrence (1915-2002) and controlled by Healy's Club. The Socialist Fellowship was formed at a fringe meeting at the 1949 Labour Party conference. It included Labour left MPs like Ellis Smith, Fenner

Brockway and Bessie Braddock and left trade union figures. Its goal was to take the Labour Party "back to socialism".

5   Follower of Michel Pablo (born Raptis, 1911-96) who led a pro-Yugoslav split in the Trotskyist movement. For a discussion of this, see Duncan Hallas, "Fourth International in decline: from Trotskyism to Pabloism 1944-1953" (1973), available at http://www.marxists.org/archive/hallas/works/1973/xx/fidecline.htm

6   Leon Trotsky, *The Revolution Betrayed* (1937).

7   By 1945 the Russian Red Army was the dominant power in Eastern Europe. Initially coalition governments presided over the old economic structures. But from late 1947 and into 1948 the local Communist Parties, resting on Russian power, moved to create replicas of the Stalinist regime in Russia across Eastern Europe. This precipitated a debate among Trotskyists about the nature of these societies.

8   Tito's communist-dominated partisan movement managed to expel the Italian and German occupiers during the Second World War through its own efforts. The regime claimed to be based on the socialist principal of self-management of the factories. But as Tito's close associate, Milovan Dijlas, revealed in his book *New Class*, Yugoslavia, like the rest of Eastern Europe, remained a class society.

9   Entrism is the view that revolutionaries should work inside the mass reformist parties to gain a wider audience.

10 "The Austin", as Longbridge was known. Herbert Austin started his motor company in 1905. In 1952 Austin and Morris Motors were merged into the British Motor Corporation and later another merger transformed it into the British Leyland Motor Corporation. In a perilous financial situation, British Leyland was nationalised in 1975. In 1988 "Rover" was sold to British Aerospace who in turn sold it to BMW in 1994. In 2000 a management buy-out by the Phoenix consortium was made of the Longbridge plant, but in 2005 it was put in the hands of the receiver. In July 2005 the Chinese corporation Nanjing Automotive bought MG Rover.

11 For much of the 1950s unemployment was virtually non-existent and there were shortages of labour.

12 Piece rates involve payment according to output rather than by the hour.

13 In the general election of February 1950 Labour gained 46.1 percent of the vote, giving it a parliamentary majority of just six. Another general election followed in October 1951 and the Tories won a majority of 19 despite Labour receiving 0.8 percent more of the vote.

14 A "bob" is an old shilling, equal to 5p now.

15 The Korean War (1950-3) was a civil war fought with international support, on the one side the United Nations (including the US and UK) and on the other Mao's China. The war ended with the country divided in two.

16 In 1956 Britain, France and Israel invaded Egypt because Nasser, the Egyptian president, had nationalised the Suez Canal. The invasion ended in humiliation for the British and signalled that the days of empire were over.

17 In 1956 there was a workers' revolution against Soviet rule in Hungary. It was brutally put down with the use of Russian tanks. See Peter Fryer's first hand account, *Hungarian Tragedy* (New Park, London, 1986).

18 *New Reasoner* (1957-60) was founded by dissident Communist Party historians E P Thompson and Christopher Hill. After merging with the *Universities and Left Review*, it became the *New Left Review*.

19 Malaya was a British colony rich in rubber and tin. Between 1948 and 1960 the British army waged a war against a communist-led national liberation movement. Malaya was granted its independence in 1957.

20 The National Liberation Front (FLN) fought a successful campaign against French rule in the Algerian War of Independence (1954-62). It was one of the key defeats for the colonial powers.

21 Ahmed Ben Bella (b 1918) was one of the leaders of the FLN who became its president shortly after independence. He was removed by a coup led by his friend Houari Boumédienne in 1965.

22 See page 45.

23 Salvadore Allende was the president of Chile (1970-3) under a left-wing Popular Front government which was deposed by General Pinochet's bloody military coup of 1973.

24 CND was formed in February 1958. It famously organised marches to Aldermaston—the first at Easter 1958. It became a mass movement between 1958 and 1963 and again in the 1980s.

25 John Baird, Labour MP (1945-64; for Wolverhampton North West, 1950-64).

26 Enoch Powell was Conservative MP for Wolverhampton South West, 1950-74. In 1968 he made the racist and inflammatory "Rivers of Blood" speech.

27 For more on the International Socialists, see the following chapter.

28 Peter Sellers in the film *I'm Alright Jack* portrayed a factory trade union convenor as a petty small-minded dictator.

29 Gracie Fields was a popular entertainer from Lancashire starring in her own films such as *Sing As We Go* (1935) and *Shipyard Sally* (1938).

30 *The Angry Silence* was a 1960 film sympathising with a character who scabs during a strike at a local factory (played by Richard Attenborough). The film vilifies the shop steward.

31 The LCDTU was formed in 1966.

32 Frank explained, "Everybody called him Burglar Bill or The Burglar. Of course stories would go around about how he got the nickname. The one I favour and I think was true was when we were working nights and we used to work a short shift on Friday nights from 6.15pm to 10.15pm. He promised to do a bit of repair work on a friend's car so he was taking a bag of tools home with him to get it done and he was stopped by a copper wanting to

know what he'd got in the bag. Bill was fed up after doing a fortnight's nights and tore into the copper a bit, with the result that he spent the weekend in the nick before he was released on the Monday."

33 *In Place of Strife* was a government White Paper put forward by Labour employment minister Barbara Castle imposing conditions on trade unions involved in industrial action, such as a ballot before action and the enforcement of settlements through an Industrial Board.

Four: The upturn and retreat

1 After successive Labour governments from 1964 the Tories unexpectedly won the 1970 general election.

2 The Industrial Relations Act of 1971 was a fresh attempt after *In Place of Strife* to shackle the trade unions legally and undermine shopfloor militancy, this time by Heath's Conservative government.

3 There had not been a national coal strike since the time of the General Strike in 1926. The 1972 and 1974 strikes were dramatic victories for the miners with high levels of rank and file activity and mass picketing.

4 As a response to the lack of coal feeding the power stations, Ted Heath imposed a three-day week (1 January-7 March 1974) in industry in order to break the miners' action.

5 Saltley was the site of a coking plant at the Birmingham gasworks. The closure of Saltley Gates by engineering workers who joined a picket by striking miners took place in early February 1972.

6 The AEU became the AEUW in

1971 after mergers with other unions.

7 For more on measured day work, see page 74.

8 Forerunner of today's Socialist Workers Party.

9 In France in May 1968 student protesters clashed with riot police. A general strike called by the unions led to a mass wave of factory occupations.

10 On 30 January 1968, the start of the Tet (New Year) festival, the Vietnamese National Liberation guerrillas launched attacks in every major city and town in South Vietnam.

11 Available in Tony Cliff, *In the Thick of Workers' Struggles: Selected Writings, Volume 2* (Bookmarks, London, 2002).

12 Cliff's point was that he was simply writing up what militant workers had told him about the situation they were facing.

13 James Burham, American former Trotskyist who developed a theory of state capitalism but in so doing supported American imperialism as a "progressive" force. By contrast, the hallmark of IS's analysis was summed up in the slogan "Neither Washington Nor Moscow, but International Socialism.".

14 The Provisional IRA bombed two pubs in Birmingham town centre, killing 19.

15 *Carworker* was a rank and file movement newspaper launched by the International Socialists. See http://www.marxists.org/archive/cliff/works/1972/08/pentonville.htm

16 For more background, see Dave Lyddon, "Survey: Measured Day Work, Piecework and British Leyland", *International Socialism*

(1st series), no 51, April-June 1972, available at http://www.marxists.org/history/etol/newspape/isj/1972/no051/lyddon.htm

17 Copies of *Carworker* can be found in the Working Class Movement Library (Salford) and at the Modern Records Centre (Warwick University) MSS.527.

18 Social contract (1974-79), nicknamed the "social con-trick", was the attempt by Harold Wilson's Labour government to impose wage restraint with the cooperation of the trade union bureaucracy, including left wingers such as Hugh Scanlon and Jack Jones.

19 Lord Ryder, *British Leyland: the Next Decade, 1975*, known as the Ryder report.

20 The Leyland Combine Committee produced the booklet that Robinson put his name to. British Leyland sacked Robinson on the grounds that it did not recognise the Combine Committee, which was an unofficial organisation opposing management plans.

21 "Steward backs Leyland in status row", the *Times*, 2 September 1976. Management observed how the shop stewards were attempting to get the 1,200 toolmakers back to work and a "senior steward" blamed the "Trots", that is the IS, for the trouble. The strike ended on 8 September after pressure from the union and the plant's stewards' committee on the toolmakers and their stewards.

22 The International Socialists became the Socialist Workers Party in 1977.

23 Right winger Terry Duffy took over from Hugh Scanlon in 1978 as president of the AEUW. He suspended the strike action in

defence of Robinson in order for the union to conduct an internal inquiry. It found in favour of the convenor but the management ignored the report and Robinson's job was lost. See the *Times*, 28 November 1979.

Afterword

1   The *Scotsman*, 15 September 2004. The highpoint was 1972 with 1.92 million units. In 2004 there were 1.7 million units.

2   "Mondism" was named after Sir Alfred Mond, chairman of ICI and a Tory, who held talks with the TUC in the wake of the defeat of the General Strike that sanctified class collaboration.

3   His anti-fascist credentials were not strong either. Churchill visited Italy in 1927 and wrote to his wife, "This country gives the impression of discipline, order, goodwill and smiling faces. A happy strict school... The fascists have been saluting in their impressive manner all over the place." He told a fascist newspaper, "If I had been an Italian, I am sure I should have been wholeheartedly with you from the start to the finish against the bestial appetites and passions of Leninism."

4   See Angus Calder, *Myth of the Blitz* (London, 1991), for more on this.

5   John Newsinger, *British Intervention and the Greek*
Revolution, p30.

6   For an account of these events, see Ilan Pappe, *The Ethnic Cleansing of Palestine* (2006, Oneworld).

7   In February 1956 the CPGB's membership was 33,095, but by February 1958 it was down to 24,670. Membership did later revive to some extent in the 1960s.

8   Tony Cliff, *State Capitalism in Russia* (Bookmarks, 1996). This analysis was first developed in 1948 as an internal document of the British Revolutionary Communist Party.

9   See Ralph Darlington and Dave Lyddon, *Glorious Summer: Class Struggle in Britain 1972* (Bookmarks, London, 2001).

10 Communist Party membership fell from 33,734 in 1965 to 28,378 in 1974 and was 20, 599 by 1979. As the shop stewards movement had grown in the 1960s, the number of CP factory branches had also fallen. In 1963 there were 263 factory branches but by 1968 this figure dropped to 182. See John Callaghan, "Industrial Militancy, 1945-79: the Failure of the British Road to Socialism", *Twentieth Century British History*, vol 15, no 4, 2004, pp388-409.

11 A useful assessment of IS's attempts at rank and file organisation can be found in Alex Callinicos, "The Rank and File Movement Today", *International Socialism* 17 (2nd series), autumn 1982.

Index

bookmarks

Britain's leading socialist bookshop for radical books
- From climate change to anti-war, from black struggle to histories of uprisings in every part of the world.
- Visit our shop or buy online to support bookselling independent of the big chains. We can also provide any title currently in print and give advice on a wide range of topics from multicultural children's books to Marxism, economics and philosophy.
- Bookmarks provides stalls at trade union conferences and campaign meetings. Let us know if you would like us to supply books for your organisation or event.

Bookmarks
1 Bloomsbury Street
London WC1B 3QE
020 7637 1848

www.bookmarks.uk.com